Read Japanese Today

READ JAPANESE TODAY

by

LEN WALSH

CHARLES E. TUTTLE COMPANY
Rutland, Vermont & Tokyo, Japan

Representatives
Continental Europe: BOXERBOOKS, INC., Zurich
British Isles: PRENTICE-HALL INTERNATIONAL, INC., London
Australasia: PAUL FLESCH & CO., PTY. LTD., Melbourne
Canada: M. G. HURTIG LTD., Edmonton

Published by the Charles E. Tuttle Company, Inc.
of Rutland, Vermont & Tokyo, Japan
with editorial offices at
Suido 1-chome, 2-6, Bunkyo-ku, Tokyo

Copyright in Japan, 1969, by Charles E. Tuttle Co., Inc.

All rights reserved

Library of Congress Catalog Card No. 69-12078

International Standard Book No. 0-8048-0496-6

First printing, 1969
Seventh printing, 1971

CONTENTS

ACKNOWLEDGEMENTS

I am indebted to Professors Takahashi Makoto, Uehara Akira and Liu Kang-Shih for their assistance in preparing this manuscript, and to Boye De Mente and Frank Hudachek for their invaluable editorial suggestions. I also wish to thank the Asia House for the research grant which made this book possible.

Tokyo, Japan
1966

SECTION ONE

CHIE TSU, published in China about 1800 years ago. For a few characters, the SHUO WEN lists more than one theory of origin. This is understandable since more than two thousand years had passed between the first invention of the characters and their compilation in the SHUO WEN lexicon and the origins of some of the characters were bound to become somewhat obscure.

Later etymologists, including some scholars from Japan, have discovered what they believe to be still other interpretations of the origin of a few of the characters. Whether the explanations of the genealogies given by the SHUO WEN CHIE TSU or the later scholars are correct is not important here in any case, since this book is not a text in etymology but a simplified method for learning the characters. Where there is a difference of opinion between the scholars, READ JAPANESE TODAY uses the interpretation which, the author hopes, will be best mnemonically for English-speaking people.

The 300 characters introduced in READ JAPANESE TODAY are grouped generally in the same categories the Chinese used as sources of the pictographs. First come the characters from nature. These are the easiest to write, probably because they were the first the Chinese invented and are therefore the most primitive and simple in construction. Next are the characters developed from parts of the human face and body. Then come characters drawn from modes of transportation, and so on.

The pronunciations given in the text for each character are limited to the most common ones. The kana which show the grammar of the word are omitted in the Japanese writing for convenience even though their equivalent is included in the roman letter transliteration. The pronunciation for the character 聞 "to hear," for example, is given in roman letters as KIKU, whereas the character 聞 actually only represents the KI sound, the root of the word. The KU sound, which is the grammatical ending representing the infinitive form of the verb, must be written in kana. The infinitive form is the one used in dictionaries so it is used in roman letters here to make it easier for you to look up these words in dictionaries later.

Japanese pronunciation is comparatively easy. Just pronounce the vowels as the Italians do—the A as in car, the E as in bed, the I as in medium, the O as in go, and the U as in luke—and the consonants as in English. Sometimes in Japanese the vowels are long, in which case they will have a line draw over the top of the letter when written in roman letters, and sometimes they are short. When you speak in Japanese just drag the long vowels out for twice the time as the short. This is often a difficult thing to do, but it is a very important distinction to make—a JŌRO is a watering pot and a JORŌ is a licensed courtesan, a SHŌJO is a young girl and a SHŌJŌ is an orangutang. For practical purposes, there is no difference in the pronunciation of these sets of words except that in one case the vowel is long and in the other it is short.

In certain cases consonants are doubled, that is, a single K becomes KK or a single P becomes PP. This is a form of abbreviation and indicates that the letter or two preceding the consonant has been dropped. The double consonant is pronounced by holding it slightly longer than a single consonant. Like the long and short vowels, this is an important distinction to make but one quite easy to effect, and you will master it with just a little practice.

One other important note on pronouncing Japanese words is that the syllables are about equally stressed, whereas in English we have some syllables which are accented. The Japanese say YO-KO-HA-MA, giving each syllable equal weight, and length, since there are no long vowels in this word, whereas we say yo-ko-HA-ma, accenting the third syllable quite strongly. When we pronounce one syllable with this extra stress, the Japanese often can not hear the other syllables. The first Americans to come to Japan told the Japanese they were a-ME-ri-cans. The Japanese couldn't hear the A sound, and thought they said "Merikens." This is why the Japanese named the wheat flour the Americans brought with them "ME-RIKEN-KO," the Japanese word for flour being KO.

The main text begins on the next page. The characters should be studied in order, since they are arranged so that those introduced in the early pages become the building-blocks for those in the later pages. There is no prescribed number to be studied at each sitting—just read as many as you have time for, then go out and see them written all around you.

To the ancient Chinese, the sun looked like this ☼, so this is the way they wrote it. They found it took too long to write the rays, however, so they shortened it to ⊙. When they changed it to its final form, to make it even easier to write and at the same time aesthetically acceptable, they squared the circle and extended the dot to a line 日.

The basic meaning of 日 is **sun**. It is used to mean **day** as well, however, in the same way that many other ancient peoples used their word for **sun** to mean **day**. 日 has several common pronunciations. When it is a word by itself it is generally pronounced HI. When it is used in compounds with other characters it is generally pronounced NICHI.

The word for **tree** the ancient Chinese first wrote like this 🌳. It was gradually simplified to 朱, and then to 木. Squared off to final form it became 木, the horizontal line representing all the branches, the vertical line the trunk, and the diagonal lines the roots. The meaning of this character is **tree** or **wood**. When it forms a word by itself it is pronounced KI, and when it is used in compounds it is pronounced MOKU.

To form the character for **root**, the Chinese just

drew in more roots, to emphasize this portion of the tree 朩 , then squared them off into a straight line 本 . In addition to the meaning **root**, this character was also used to mean **origin** or **source**. The meaning was later extended to mean **book** also, which the Chinese felt to be the root or source of knowledge. When 本 is used alone to form a word it is usually pronounced HON. When it is used in compounds it can be pronounced either HON or MOTO.

The compound formed by putting **root** or **origin** 本 together with the character for sun 日 is 日 本 , origin-of-the-sun, pronounced NIPPON or NIHON, which is what the Japanese call their country. This compound would normally be pronounced NICHIHON, but the Japanese abbreviate it to either NIPPON or NIHON.

A picture of the sun in the east at sunrise rising up behind a tree 東 was the scene the Chinese selected to mean **east**. In this new character they wrote tree 木 and sun 日 in the same way they wrote them when they were used as separate characters. The final form of **east** became 東 . Used by itself, it is pronounced HIGASHI. Where it appears in compounds, as in TŌKYŌ, it is pronounced TŌ. It is not the TO in KYŌTO, however, although the KYŌ is the same in both. The TŌ in TŌKYŌ has a long Ō, while the TO in KYŌTO has a short O. When used in family names 東 is sometimes pronounced AZUMA. The Governor of Tokyo (1967) is Governor 東 AZUMA.

The KYŌ in TŌKYŌ was originally a picture of a stone lantern 高 . These lanterns were placed at the gates of the Chinese Emperor's residence and later at the gates of the Imperial City. The lanterns came therefore to symbolize the nation's capital, so the Chinese adopted a pictograph of the stone lantern to mean **capital**. They first wrote it 京 . Now it is written 京 , and pronounced KYŌ or KEI. TŌKYŌ, 東 京 , therefore, means Eastern Capital.

The Chinese decided to use a picture of a bird's wings, which to them looked like this 羽 , to mean **wings**. Their pictograph of this was first 羽 , later squared off to 羽 . This character means **wing**, a wing of anything that flies: bird, butterfly, angel, or airplane. It is pronounced HANE, and is the first character in the compound HANEDA, the name of Tokyo's airport.

The DA in the compound HANEDA means **rice-paddy**. The paddies looked like this so the Chinese first drew them 井 . The final form was 田 . This character is pronounced TA, although sometimes it is changed to DA when it is easier to pronounce that way. HANEDA is written 羽 田 , Winged-Field. The well-known HONDA motorcycle company writes its name 本 田 Original-Paddy.

A strong hand bearing down on things represented to the Chinese the idea of strength or power. Drawing in all the fingers took too much time, so they abstracted the form of the hand and drew 人 . Squaring this, they produced the final form 力 . It means **strength** or **power,** and is pronounced CHIKARA when used alone, and RYOKU or RIKI when used in compounds.

The Chinese added power 力 to a rice-paddy 田 , and made the character for **man** 男 . This character is pronounced OTOKO when used alone and DAN when used in compounds. It signifies the male man, not the species man, which will appear on the next page.

A **woman** the Chinese saw as a pregnant young thing seated with her arms outstretched 女. This was later written 女, and finally 女. It is pronounced ONNA when used by itself, and JO in compounds. The characters man 男, and woman 女 appear on the doors of all those places with limited entrance to one or the other.

Mother to the Chinese was a woman 女 with her breasts drawn in. They pictured her first as 母, then added a hat to give her balance 母. The final form of this character is 母. Used by itself it is generally pronounced (with the addition of several kana which indicate respect) OKĀSAN. This is the most popular Japanese word for mother, but to be understood it must be pronounced with a distinctly long A—OKAAASAN—to distinguish it from OKASAN, which means Mr. Oka. In compounds it is pronounced BO.

Person, the species man, a general word which can refer to either man, woman, or child, the Chinese pictured as the human form in general 人. This was written in final form like this 人. It is pronounced HITO when used by itself, and NIN or JIN when used in compounds. It is the JIN in NIHONJIN 日 本 人 , which means Japan-person, or Japanese. An AMERIKA-JIN is an America-person, an American. There are no characters for the name "America" so it is written in phonetic (kana) letters.

Since every man 人 had a mother 母 , the Chinese combined these two characters into one 每 to produce the meaning **every**. When two characters or pictographs are combined to form a new character, either one or both of them may change shape or proportion slightly in order to fit into the square. Writing 含 would be unwieldly and un-aesthetic, so the Chinese changed the shape of man to 𠂉 and wrote the character **every** 每 . The pronounciation is MAI. The word 每 日 MAINI-CHI, in addition to meaning "every day" or "daily," is also the name of a major Japanese newspaper.

The character for **child** the Chinese formed from a picture of a swaddled baby 𨸏 . They first wrote this character 孑 , then squared it into final form 子 . It is pronounced KO. A 子 KO is a child. An 男 ノ 子 OTOKO-NO-KO, man-child, is a boy, and an 女ノ子 ONNA-NO-KO, woman-child, is a girl. In both these words the NO, which simply indicates the conjunctive case, is written, as all grammatical indicators are, in kana. 子 KO is also used as the last character in almost all Japanese girls' names, where it means "sweet little....."

A woman 女 and a child 子 together signified love and goodness to the Chinese. They combined these two pictographs into the new character 好, which means **love** or **goodness.**

When used as a verb, meaning **to love** or **to like,** it is generally pronounced SUKU. This is frequently abbreviated to SUKI, which means simply "I like it" or "I like you." When used as an adjective, where it means **good** or **nice,** it is generally pronounced II.

A man standing with his arms stretched out as far as he can manage 大 was the Chinese conception of bigness. Their early writings show it drawn 大 Now it is drawn 大 . This character means **big.** Used by itself it is pronounced ŌKII. In compounds with other characters it is pronounced Ō or DAI. 大 日本 DAI-NIHON or DAI-NIPPON means Greater Japan. 大田 ŌTA, Big-Paddy, is the name of one of the wards in Tokyo as well as being a family name. 大木 ŌKI, Big-Tree, is a family name.

The same man, standing this time with his arms pulled in toward his sides 人 signified smallness. The Chinese wrote it first 小 , and then in final form 小 . It means **small**. By itself it is pronounced CHIISAI. In compounds it is pronounced KO or SHŌ, and sometimes, in proper names, O.

Just plain standing is represented by a man standing, this time not in the abstract but on the ground 立 . It was originally written 立 , now it is written 立 . It means **to stand** or **to rise up**. When used by itself, it is pronounced TATSU. In compounds it is pronounced RITSU or, in a few cases, TACHI. The well known Japanese electrical equipment manufacturer, HITACHI, writes its name 日 立 , Sun-Rise.

The next three characters are **one** —— **two** ═ **three** ≡ . Up to three, the Chinese allowed one line per unit, one for one —— , two for two ═ and three for three ≡ . They are pronounced —— ICHI, ═ NI, ≡ SAN.

The number **five** began the same way 二 but this had too many horizontal lines to write in a small space, so the Chinese took two of the lines and made them vertical 廾 . Then they opened up one corner for balance and wrote it 五 . This is pronounced GO and means **five**.

Ten was taken from the ten fingers of two crossed hands 🖐 . It is now written 十 , and pronounced JŪ. 十 人 JŪNIN means ten people.

The Chinese tripled power 力 力 力 then multiplied by ten 十 to form the character 協 , many strengths together, meaning **to unite , to join together in cooperation.** 協 is pronounced KYŌ. The compound 協 力 KYŌRYOKU, unite-strength, means cooperation.

From a view of a flowing river 〰 the Chinese drew the character for river 〰 . In final form they straightened it to 川 . This is pronounced KAWA, sometimes changed to GAWA for euphony. TACHI-KAWA, a city near Tokyo which contains an American airbase, writes its name 立 川 Rising-River.
川 also appears in family names :

立 川 TACHIKAWA Rising-River. This is a family name as well as a geographical name.

大 川 ŌKAWA Big-River

小 川 OGAWA Small-River

The Chinese found that if you squeeze a river 氺 you get water. They wrote the character for **water** therefore first as 氺 , and finally 水 . By itself it is pronounced MIZU, and in compounds generally SUI. One exception to the pronunciation in compounds is the word 大 水 , big-water, meaning flood, where it is pronounced ŌMIZU.

To signify the meaning **enter**, the Chinese selected a picture of a smaller river flowing into a larger 从 . In final form the rivers became lines, written 入 . By itself it is pronounced IRERU when it is used in the transitive case, where it means **to enter**, and pronounced HAIRU when used in the intransitive case, where it means **to be entered** or **to contain**. In compounds it is pronounced NYŪ. This character will almost always appear above entrance-ways to such public places as train stations, hotels, and department stores. Sometimes it appears alone 入 , but most often in a compound with 口 , which is the character for **mouth** or **opening**.

Mouth or **opening** ⬭ was first written ⊔
Then, with little alteration, its final form became □
When used alone it is pronounced KUCHI. In compounds it is usually pronounced KŌ, but in some cases the pronounciation KUCHI, often changed to GUCHI for euphony, is used also. Many train stations have a
東 □ HIGASHI-GUCHI, east entrance. 入
□ IRIGUCHI, enter-opening, means entrance.

A mouth □ with a line through the middle 中 means **middle** or **inside**. It is pronounced either NAKA or CHŪ. Besides being a common word in daily speech it is used extensively in names of people and places. Some family names in which it appears are:

中	田	NAKADA	Middle-Field
田	中	TANAKA	Field-Middle
中	川	NAKAGAWA	Middle-River
川	中	KAWANAKA	River-Middle
中	立	CHŪRITSU	middle-standing. This means neutral.
日	中	NITCHŪ	middle-of-the-day. This means during the

day. This should be pronounced NICHI-CHŪ, but it is abbreviated to NITCHŪ.

女 中 JOCHŪ girl-inside. This is a housemaid.

The mouth with a line through the middle 中 means **middle** with the connotation "inside." The Chinese invented another character to mean **middle** with the connotation "center," that is, the **exact middle.** They drew a circle ○ around the middle or the center of a man with arms outstretched 大 and formed the character 央 . Later, they squared the circle 央 and finally dropped the bottom half of the square for clarity 央 . This is pronounced Ō. It is never used by itself and does not appear in many compounds. One of its compounds, 中 央 , middle-middle, meaning **middle** or **center,** however, can be seen quite often. Tokyo station has a 中 央 ☐ CHŪŌ-GUCHI, central-entrance. Tokyo has a 中 央 CHŪŌ Railroad Line and also a 中 央 CHŪŌ Ward.

The sun 日 combined with center 央 forms

a character which means **to reflect an image on** 映 .
This character is used in reference to taking a picture,
duplicating a document on a copying machine, screen-
ing a film, reflecting an image in a mirror: in short, in
any case where an image is transferred from one place
to another. It is pronounced UTSUSU, the transitive
case, and UTSURU, the intransitive case, when it is
used by itself. It is pronounced EI in compounds.

映 is used in a compound with the character for
picture or **boundary** to form the word for movies. The
character for **picture** or **boundary** was formed from a
picture of a rice paddy 田 with a frame or boundary
line around it ☐ . The character was first written
画 , then in final form 画 . At first, it meant **draw
a boundary line around.** Later, since a picture had a
boundary line or border around it, the character was
also used to mean **picture.** In modern times it still
means either **picture** or **boundary.** An 映画 EIGA,
reflected-picture, is a movie. Two of Japan's largest
movie studios, which also own a chain of theaters of
the same name, are 大映 DAIEI, Big-Reflection,
and 東映 TŌEI, Eastern-Reflection. A 日本
画 NIHONGA, Japan-picture, is a Japanese paint-
ing, as distinguished from Western, or oil, paintings.

The character for mouth ☐ is used occasionally to mean **a person,** similar to the English usage in the phrase, "too many mouths to feed." In the character 古 the ☐ stands for a whole generation of people. The ─┼─ on top of the ☐ is the character for ten, and the whole character signifies "ten generations." The Chinese interpreted this to mean **old.** By itself 古 is pronounced FURUI, and in compounds KO. It is sometimes used in family names: 古 田 FURUTA, Old-Field; 古 川 FURUKAWA, Old-River.

The Chinese took three **mouths** or **openings** ☐☐☐ here referring to the openings of boxes, and piled them up 品 to indicate many boxes. They used this character to mean **goods** or **things.** It is pronounced SHINA or HIN. In a compound with 中 CHŪ, middle, and 古 KO, old, it forms the word 中 古 品 CHŪKOHIN, middle-old-things, or second-hand goods. 品 川 SHINAGAWA is the name of a Ward in Tokyo. 品 川 , sometimes abbreviated to 品 , appears on many automobile license plates in Tokyo to show that they were issued at the Shinagawa Vehicle Registration Bureau, one of four in Tokyo.

Three mouths □□□ inside a boundary 區 forms the character 區, which symbolizes many mouths inside a boundary. This character means **ward** or **district** or **section**, almost always in reference to a geographical division. 品 川 區 SHINAGAWA-KU is Shinagawa Ward; 中 央 區 CHŪO-KU is Chuo Ward; and 大 田 區 ŌTA-KU is Ota Ward.

Another geographical division, smaller than a 區, is a 町. This character is formed from a picture of a rice paddy 田 with a sign in front 丁 giving it a name. It is pronounced MACHI or CHŌ, and means a **town** or a **section of a ward.** Each 區 KU, or Ward will generally have many 町 CHŌ, or Sections.

The sign 丁 alone also forms a character. It means basically a **unit of measure,** and is pronounced CHŌ also. Most of the 町 CHŌ in any city are further sub-divided into numbered CHŌME, for example: ITCHŌME, No. 1 CHŌME; NICHŌME, No. 2 CHŌME; SANCHŌME, No. 3 CHŌME. The CHŌ in this CHŌME is written 丁, while the ME is the character for **eye**, which will be introduced on page 71

A mouth ▢ speaking its lines ☰ forms the character 言, which means **to say**. It is pronounced YŪ.

A man 人 and his sayings 言 put together 人言 mean **trust**. When two characters or pictographs are combined to form a new character, as we saw in 毎 MAI, **every**, one of them may change its shape so the final character can be written in a reasonable space with reasonable clarity, beauty and balance. In 毎 MAI, **man** 人 changed shape to ⼃ since it appears at the top of the square; in **"trust"** man changes to ⼂ since it appears at the side of the square. The final form of **trust** therefore is 信. This is pronounced SHIN. It is a common character in the financial world since it is used in Japanese to mean the **trust** in Savings & Trust, which is as popular a name for banking institutions in Japanese as it is in English.

Saying 言 in tens 十 means **counting** or **measuring** 計. This character appears over the cashier's counter in each restaurant or store, where it means **counting**. It is used on all types of measuring instruments, from thermometers to computers, where it means **measuring.** On instruments, the other characters appearing with 計 indicate what kind of measuring instrument it is, while the 計 can be translated as -**meter.** 計 is pronounced KEI in all these compounds, and HAKARU when used by itself.

A mouth ☐ with a tongue 川 sticking out, drawn slightly forked 舌 means tongue. This is pronounced SHITA.

The Chinese understood that to talk requires more glibness than to say, so they added tongue 舌 to say 言 to make **talk** 話. The difference between say 言 and talk 話 in Japanese is about the same as in English: "take me home, she **said**", and "**talk** on the telephone." This character is pronounced HANASU when used by itself and WA in compounds.

A moist tongue was a sign of life, in China, so the Chinese added the character for water 水 to the character for tongue 舌 to form the character for life or energy.

When water 水 is combined with other characters, it changes shape considerably. The change proceeds from 水 to ⺡ then ⺡ and finally ⺡. This pictograph is used very frequently as a building-block for other characters, and each character in which it is used is related to water or liquid in some way.

The final form of **life** or **energy**, therefore, is 活. It is pronounced KATSU · 日活 NIKKATSU, Sun-Life, is the name of another of Japan's movie empires, which also owns the 日活 NIKKATSU Hotel in downtown Tokyo.

A **word** or **language** was something said 言 by five 五, signifying many, mouths 口. The Chinese wrote the final character 語. It is pronounced GO. 日本語 NIHONGO, Japan-Language, means of course the Japanese language.

For **up** and **down**, the Chinese began with dots above and below a centerline, 上 and 下. To make it easier to write and easier to recognize, they expanded the dot to a vertical line and added a handle. 上, meaning up or **on top of**, is pronounced UE when used by itself and JO in compounds. 下, meaning **down** or **below**, is pronounced SHITA when **used** by itself, and GE in compounds.

上 and 下 can be used as verbs also, in which case they mean **go up** or **put up**, and **go down** or **put down.** As a verb, 上 is pronounced AGARU or AGERU, and 下 is pronounced SAGARU or SAGERU. 下 has the additional pronunciation of KUDARU or KUDASU, here with the connotation give down, from which came the word KUDASAI, **give down to me.** This is generally translated into English as "please give me......," and is a very important word in Japanese.

Some compounds using 上 and 下 are:

上 映 中　JŌEICHŪ　upon-screen-middle-of. This sign appears on movie posters at all theaters, and means "Now Playing."

下 水　GESUI　down-water. Sewerage.

下 町　SHITAMACHI　down-town. This means downtown.

上 and 下 are used in proper names also:

川 上　KAWAKAMI　Upper-River

上 田　UEDA　Upper-Field

下 田　SHIMODA　Lower-Field. Besides being a family name, Shimoda is the name of the town south of Tokyo where Admiral

Perry landed, first opening Japan to Western influences after more than 200 years of isolation.

The character for **mountain** was taken from a picture of a range of mountains with three peaks. The Chinese first drew it ⁄⁀⁄. Then each peak became a line, and the character for **mountain** became 山. It is pronounced YAMA or SAN. It is of course the SAN in FUJISAN, Mount Fuji. Like all words of nature, 山 is a favorite character of the Japanese for family names:

山 下	YAMASHITA	Below-the-Mountain
山 川	YAMAKAWA	Mountain-Stream
大 山	ŌYAMA	Big-Mountain
山 中	YAMANAKA	Amidst-the-Mountains. This is also the name for one of the famous Fuji five lakes.
山 本	YAMAMOTO	Original-Mountain
山 一	YAMAICHI	First-Mountain. This is the name of one of the largest brokerage houses in Japan.

There are many, many more. 山 is also a favorite of Sumo wrestlers. Many of the Japanese Sumo wrestlers use YAMA in their professional name.

An opening 口 in a mountain range 𝅗𝅥 signifies a **valley**. The mountain range was first written 𝅘𝅥 then ∧∧. The final character is 谷. It is generally pronounced TANI, but sometimes in proper names it is pronounced YA. The Ōtani Hotel writes its name 大 谷, Big-Valley.

A mountain cliffside ⌐ with a stone below ◯ was the Chinese pictograph for **stone**. They first wrote it ⌐◯ then in final form 石. It is sometimes written 石 also. Written either way, it is pronounced ISHI by itself and SEKI in compounds. 石 is also often used in proper names:

石 田　ISHIDA　　Stone-Field
石 川　ISHIKAWA　Stone-River

The character for **oil** is a picture of a field 田 with a derrick sticking out 田. To indicate that what was taken from the ground was liquid, the character for water 水, abbreviated 氵, was added. The final character is written 油. It is pronounced

ABURA by itself and YU in compounds. 石油 SEKIYU, rock-oil, is petroleum. The name of almost all the gas stations in Japan contain the name of the company which owns them followed by the word 石油 SEKIYU. Nihon Petroleum Corporation's stations all have signs reading 日本石油 NIHON SEKIYU. Those owned by Daikyo Petroleum Corporation have signs reading 大協石油 DAIKYŌ SEKIYU.

油 also refers to any other type of oil in liquid form. Each bottle of cooking oil for example, will have 油 printed on the label, and so will each bottle of shoyu, the sauce the Japanese put on all their food. 油 is the second character in shoyu, which is made from soybean oil. The first character has not been introduced yet.

A picture of a quarter-moon 🌙 became the character for **moon**. The Chinese wrote it first like this 🌙 then squared it off and gave it balance 月 . It is pronounced TSUKI when used alone , and GETSU or GATSU in compounds. Like sun 日 , it is used to measure time as well as to signify itself. A sun 日 is a day, and a moon 月 is a month. The names of the months are formed from the numbers 1 through

12 combined with moon 月 pronounced GATSU.
一 月 ICHIGATSU is January, 二 月 NI-
GATSU is February, 三 月 SANGATSU is March,
十 月 JŪGATSU is October.

A picture of the full moon rising from behind a
mountain in early evening  formed the character
for **evening**. The Chinese first drew it 夕 , then
abstracted it to 夕 . It is pronounced YŪ or YŪBE.

夕 is combined with a divining rod 卜 , which
in ancient China was used by the diviners or fortune-
tellers and therefore signifies diviner or fortune-teller,
to form the character 外. This new character
means **outside,** the Chinese reasoning that diviners
or fortune-tellers were night-people and therefore
had to operate outside under the moonlight. It is pronounced SOTO or HOKA when used by itself and GAI
in compounds. It means **outside, outdoors,** or **besides.**
A 外 人 GAIJIN, outside-person, is a foreigner.

Evening 夕 combined with mouth 口 , here indicating an open mouth calling out a name, gave the
Chinese the character for **name** 名 . It was developed from the practice of the ancient Chinese sen-

tries who at night had to hear the name of the approaching citizen called out before he would pass him. It is pronounced NA when used by itself and MEI in compounds. A 名 人 MEIJIN, name-person, is one who has a name, a famous person. A 名 画 MEIGA, name-picture, is a famous picture, a masterpiece. On most application blanks, you write your name on the line marked 名 NA.

A moon rising from behind a mountain 夕 added to another moon rising from behind a mountain 多 makes many moons. The American Indians counted in many moons, and so did the early Chinese. Later, however, the Chinese dropped the moons and just left many. The character 多 now means **many.** It is pronounced ŌI when used by itself and TA in compounds. You will see 多 on many automobile license plates in Tokyo since TA is the abbreviation for TAMAGAWA, which is the name of another of the four Vehicle Registration Bureaus in Tokyo.

The moon, this time the moon by itself 月, combined with sun 日 means **bright.** The completed character is written 明 and is pronounced AKARUI when used by itself and MEI in compounds.

The Chinese saw the sun as ☀ then removed the rays and wrote ⊙ for sun. They took the rays and pulled them together ✳ to form the character for **rays**. In final form they squared and balanced off these lines to 光. This characters means rays of light, either the natural rays of the sun or stars, or the reflected rays of any polished surface. It also mean **to shine, to sparkle.** When used by itself it is pronounced HIKARU or HIKARI; when used in compounds it is pronounced KŌ. 日 光 NIKKŌ, Sun-Shine, is the name of a popular resort town near Tokyo. In family names 光 is sometimes pronounced MITSU.

The next few characters were formed basically from pictures of plants and trees.

A picture of the sun at dawn rising over a field of flowers symbolized to the Chinese the meaning **early.** This picture soon came to be represented by the sun and one flower. The sun had already been squared to 日. The flower was squared to 十 and the final character became 早. It is pronounced HAYAI. The Japanese use this word also for the meaning **fast** or **quick.** It is also used to write, with the addition of the proper kana, OHAYŌ, which is the Japanese word for good-morning, literally "it is early."

For the word **morning**, the Chinese wanted to use a picture of the sun rising at dawn over a field of flowers placed beside the moon which had just been out all night 月 . They had already decided that , abbreviated 早 , meant **early**, however, so if they put this together with moon the new character 朝 would show the concept **early moon** instead of **morning**. The Chinese therefore added one more flower above the sun to differentiate it from 早 , then added 卓 to moon 月 to form the character for **morning** 朝 . This is pronounced ASA. 朝 日 ASAHI, the **morning-sun** or **rising-sun**, is a very popular name for business firms in Japan.

A flower sprouting from the earth means **earth**. The flower, as we saw above, was squared to 十 , so the final character became 土 . This is pronounced TSUCHI by itself and TO or DO in compounds. 土 木 DOBOKU, (this should be pronounced DOMOKU, but it is changed to DOBOKU for euphony) earth-and-wood, means essentially "civil engineering". Many construction firms use this as part of their company name: 山 川 土 木 YAMA-KAWA DOBOKU is in English the Yamakawa Civil Engineering Company.

When the ground supports a flower coming out in full bloom 𝄞 the emphasis in meaning changes from "the ground" to "the act of coming out." The meaning of this character, first written ⚓ and finally 出 , is **coming out**. It is the opposite of **going in** 入 , which as you remember is a picture of a small river flowing into a larger one. 出 is pronounced DERU when used by itself, and DE or SHUTSU in compounds. A 出 口 DEGUCHI, coming-out-mouth, means exit. Each railroad or subway wicket will have the two directions pointed out with signs: 出 口 DEGUCHI for exit, and 入 口 IRIGUCHI for entrance.

When the flower is pictured at its peak of growth ready to give birth to another cycle of life 𝄞 the emphasis in meaning shifts again—to **birth**. The Chinese first wrote this character 生 and later 生 . Often you will still see it written 生 but in modern times it is usually abbreviated further to 生 This character has many meanings, though these all evolve quite naturally from the basic meaning indicated by the picture: giving birth.

生 has about 22 different pronunciations, and unlike most of the other characters, the meaning changes with the pronunciation. Pronounced UMU it means **give birth,** pronounced UMARERU it means **to be born.** Pronounced NAMA it means **raw.** Pronounced SEI it means **life.** In many beer halls you will see the sign 生, in this case pronounced NAMA. Here it is the abbreviation for NAMA Beer— **raw** beer or draft beer.

When the rice plants have flowered, the grains are harvested and the stalks are cut. The stalks are bundled, tied and stacked and look like this 卌 . The first drawing of these bundled stacks, which the Chinese used as the character for **rice,** was 꽃 , and the final form was 米 By itself this is pronounced KOME; in compounds BEI. It means **rice,** the rice you buy in a grain store, already harvested but not yet cooked. Pronounced BEI it also is the character the Japanese use to write America.

A picture of a single grain of rice 白 was selected by the Chinese to symbolize the color **white.** They

wrote it first ⏜ and finally squared it off to 白
This is pronounced SHIROI when used by itself and
HAKU in compounds.

A single tree 木 means **tree**. Two of them together 林 mean **woods**. Three of them together
森 mean **forest**. 林 is pronounced HAYASHI,
and 森 is pronounced MORI. Both are very popular
in family names:

林	HAYASHI	Woods
森	MORI	Forest
大 林	ŌBAYASHI	Big-Woods
小 林	KOBAYASHI	Little-Woods
大 森	ŌMORI	Big-Forest
小 森	KOMORI	Little-Forest
森 山	MORIYAMA	Forest-Mountain

A picture of a tree 木 is tree. A picture of a tree
bearing fruit 柴 is **fruit**. This character was first
written by the Chinese 果 and finally 果. This
picture looks very much like a tree 木 farm 田,
but it is not. If tree-farm helps you remember it, you
may call it that, but it is actually a tree bearing fruit.
It is pronounced KA, and means **fruit**. By extension
it also means fruit of your effort, **result**.

The earliest confections in China were made from fruit or berries or nuts. The Chinese added the pictograph for plants or bushes 艹, on which the nuts and berries grew, to the pictograph for fruit 果 to form the character for confectionery 菓. This also is pronounced KA. It refers to any type of confection—cakes, cookies, rice cookies, Japanese sweet bean cakes, sweetmeats, etc. 菓 子 KASHI, little-confection, is the popular word confectionery. All the pastry shops have this sign out front.

A man 人 resting beside a tree 木 is the character for **rest**. It is written 休 and pronounced YASUMU by itself and KYŪ in compounds. This is the character a shopkeeper will put on his door on holidays to indicate he's closed.

Man 人 and root 本 together form the character 体, root-of-man, meaning the **human body.** Occasionally, by extension, this character refers to a body of men, for example a group or delegation. It is pronounced KARADA by itself and TAI in compounds.

The next few characters have their origins in the shape and actions of the human hand.

A **hand** itself 𝙼 was first written by the Chinese ⼿ , and gradually evolved ⼿ ⼿ to 手 , the final form. This means **hand,** and is pronounced TE.

Two hands reaching out to clasp each other 𝕊𝕊 mean **friend.** The Chinese first drew these hands omitting a few fingers to save time ⼷. They later straightened out the lines 友 , then finally squared it off to 友 . This is pronounced either TOMO or YŪ. This is the TOMO in the word TOMODACHI, meaning friend. The DACHI is written in kana.

The character for **left** is a hand holding a carpenter's ruler. Carpenters usually hold the ruler in their left hand and draw the line with their right. The left hand, abbreviated 𠂇 as we saw in 友 TOMO, was combined with the ruler ＼ , which was written first 」 and finally 工 , to give the final form 左 . This is pronounced HIDARI by itself and SA in compounds.

The carpenter's ruler 工 is itself a character. It is pronounced KU or KŌ, and has the meaning **to build** or **builder.** A 大 工 DAIKU, big-builder, is a carpenter. 人 工 JINKŌ, man-built, means man-made, not natural, as in man-made satellite or man-made harbor.

Right is written with a hand 𝖸 and a mouth ☐, signifying the hand you eat with, the right. Its final form is 右. It is pronounced MIGI by itself and U in compounds. It refers only to the direction **right**; it has nothing to do with the right in rights-and-duties.

A hand 𠂇 holding what appears to be the moon 有 means **to have, to exist**. Actually, the hand is holding a piece of meat ⬯ and not the moon. The Chinese drew the piece of meat like this 內, and then in final form 肉. This character alone 肉 means **meat**, and appears on every butcher shop window. It is pronounced NIKU. When using it as a building-block in other characters, however, the Chinese compressed its shape from 肉 to 內, and finally to 月. Unfortunately, this is written just as moon is. 有 is pronounced ARU by itself and YŪ in compounds. To be 有名 YŪMEI, have-name, means to be famous.

A picture of a hand 𝖸 with a dot ヽ measuring how far the pulse is from the wrist 𝖸 means **measure**. The Chinese first wrote it 𝖸, then in final form 寸. It is pronounced SUN. As it does in English, this word "measure" has two meanings: measure of distance and measure of justice. In its first meaning it is approximately equivalent to our inch — one SUN is 1.13 inches. In its second meaning, it refers to law.

In modern times when 寸 is used as a separate character it means measure of distance, and when it is used as a building-block for other characters it means measure of justice, law.

Combining **law** 寸 with tree 木, here symbolizing jungle, forms the character 村, **village,** that form of social organization which brings law out of the jungle. It is pronounced MURA by itself and SON in combinations. 村 is used as a part of the name of many villages, as we use ....Village, -ville, or -ton. It is also very popular as a family name:

中村	NAKAMURA	Middle-Village
下村	SHIMOMURA	Lower-Village
本村	MOTOMURA	Original-Village
田村	TAMURA	Paddy-Village
木村	KIMURA	Tree-Village

A roof was 𠆢 written by the Chinese 宀. Placing the pictograph for **law** 寸 under a roof 宀 forms 守, which means **guard.** By itself this is pronounced MAMORU, and in compounds SHU. You will see this character, sometimes alone and sometimes alongside one or two other characters, on the door to guard houses, the watchman's office in building basements, and sentry posts.

Placing the pictograph for **law** 寸 under the pictograph for **earth** 土 , here indicating "place," forms 寺 , symbolizing a place where laws are made, meaning **temple.** This is pronounced TERA by itself and JI in compounds. 寺 is usually the last character in the two or three characters which form the names of temples in Japan, the first one or two characters telling of course whose temple it is. The famous 東 大 寺 TŌDAIJI in Nara is the Great-Eastern Temple. 寺 is used occasionally in family names:

山 寺 YAMADERA   Mountain-Temple
寺 本 TERAMOTO   Temple-Origin

The character for temple 寺 combined with the character for say 言 forms 詩 , temple-speaking, meaning **poetry** or **poem.** This is pronounced SHI.

The character for temple 寺 combined with the character for sun 日 forms 時 , which means **time** or **hour.** It was the temple in the early days which measured the travel of the sun and kept the calendar. By itself 時 is pronounced TOKI, and in compounds JI. It is the JI in NAN JI DESS KA, meaning "what time is it?" It is also the JI in 一 時 ICHIJI, 二 時 NIJI, 三 時 SANJI, meaning one o'clock, two o'clock, three o'clock. It is combined with 計 KEI, to measure, to form the word 時 計 , hour-measure, or clock. Here 時 takes the special pronounciation TO, and the word for clock is pronounced TOKEI.

The character for temple 寺 combined with the character for hand 手, which is here changed in shape to 扌 so it can be fitted into a square with temple, forms 持 . This means **to have** or **to hold** or **to own,** since in the early days it was only the temple which could own anything. By itself it is pronounced MOTSU and in compounds JI.

The pictograph 寸 , here indicating "hand," held up against a man 人 means to **hold up against** or **attach.** The character is written 付 . It is generally used as a verb, pronounced TSUKU or TSUKERU, but the verb stem, TSUKI, is often seen on menus or ads, where it means "with....", as for example "with bath" or "with rice."

A hand held out ⼺ receiving a baton ⌐ from another hand 𝄈 forms the character 受 , meaning to **receive**. The final form of the bottom hand is 又 , the same as that in 友 TOMO, friend. The baton stays as it is, and the upper hand is reduced to its bare outline ⼍ .The final character is written 受 . It is generally pronounced UKERU by itself and JU in compounds. In combination with the verb 付 TSUKERU, however, its pronunciation is reduced to the verb stem UKE, while TSUKERU is reduced to TSUKE. The new word 受付 UKETSUKE, receive-attach, means reception or receptionist, and will be seen on a little sign on reception desks in almost every building in Japan. On many buildings still under construction there will be large signs placed on the outside walls 受付中 UKE-TSUKECHŪ, reception-middle, meaning "in the process of accepting applications." This indicates that there is space for rent.

The same two hands 受 and the baton ⌐ , when joined together in another way have a different meaning. Where one hand has hold of the baton and is tugging it away from the other 爰 , it means **struggle** or **dispute**. The final form is 爭 , pronounced ARASOU by itself and SŌ in compounds.

Two hands joined in holding up a ball together 𥄉 means **together**. The Chinese first squared it off to 吕, and finally 共 . It is pronounced KYŌ. 共立 KYŌRITSŪ, together-stand, means **cooperative** or **joint** or **common**.

Two hands 彐 ⺕ pouring some knowledge 爻, represented by two Xes, into the head of a child 子 seated inside a building 冖 is the character for **learning**. The final form of the character, with the hands slightly modified to ⺕ ⺕, is 學 . This is pronounced MANABU by itself and GAKU in compounds. A 學生 GAKUSEI, learning-being, is a student. A 大學 DAIGAKU, great-learning, is a university, and a 大學生 DAIGAKUSEI is a university student. 東京大學 TŌKYŌ DAIGAKU is Tokyo University, often abbreviated to 東大 TŌDAI.

A hand 屮 holding up a branch 丵 means either

hold up or **branch. Branch** in this case, however, refers to any thing branched off from the main stem rather than simply a branch of a tree. The branch was originally written 屮 then finally 十. The completed character is 支, pronounced SHI. It is used to indicate branch offices, branch stores, branches of organizations. 支持 SHIJI, hold-up-hold, means to support.

To indicate a branch of a tree, the pictograph for tree 木 is added to the character for **branch** 支, forming the new character 枝. This is pronounced EDA.

A hand holding a brush 🖌 writing on a piece of paper 📄 is the character for **write**. The Chinese first wrote it 𦘒 then 書 finally 書. This character is pronounced KAKU by itself and SHO in compounds. In addition to the meaning **write** it also means **writing** or **written things,** and in this sense it appears in the name of almost every bookshop in Japan.

In 書 the brush is pointed downward, writing. When it is pointed upward, poised and ready to record things as they happen 事, it forms the character for **thing** or **happening** or **affair.** The Chinese first wrote this 事 then 事 and finally 事. It is pronounced KOTO or JI. Some examples of its application are:

工 事 KŌJI   build-things. This means construction.

工 事 中 KŌJICHŪ construction-middle. This means Under Construction. You can see this written on signs at all the road construction sites.

人 事 JINJI   People-affairs. This means human affairs. It is also the name of the Personnel Section in business firms and government offices.

時 事 JIJI   time-things. This means current events. One of the leading Japanese news services is called 時 事 JIJI Press.

To form the character for **oppose** or **anti-**, the Chinese used a picture of a hand 又 and a picture of a hill ╱ to indicate a hand-made hill, piled up in opposition to the progress of your enemy. This was written in final form 反 and is pronounced HAN. Most of the placards carried by demonstrators in Japan will have 反 written on them, since these demonstrators usually are campaigning against something. Some other examples are:

反語 HANGO oppose-word. This means irony.

反共 HANKYŌ This means anti-communist. KYŌ is the abbreviation for KYŌSANSHUGISHA, which means communist.

When the Chinese wanted to indicate an actual hill, they added earth 土 to the man-made hill, forming the character 坂, meaning **hill** or **slope.** This is pronounced SAKA.

This completes the section on hands for now, although there are in the Japanese lexicon many other characters originating from pictures of the hands and their actions.

The next group of characters have their origin in pictures of the feet.

A picture of the foot 𝔚 drawn first 𝕾 then 𝕾 and finally squared off to 止, means **stop**. By itself it is pronounced TOMARU, the transitive form, or TOMERU, the intransitive form. In compounds it is pronounced SHI. 止 appears on all the traffic stop signs, sometimes with other characters and sometimes alone. Written with the word for middle 中 it forms the new word 中 止 CHŪSHI, stopped-in-the-middle, meaning suspended or cancelled. 中 止 CHŪSHI will be posted for example on a theater or hall where a performance has been cancelled.

While a picture of the foot 止 means stop, a picture of the leg 𝓵 rneans **foot**. Actually, in Japanese this character is used for either **leg** or **foot**. This greatly complicates the explanation to your doctor that you have a pain in the 𝓵 . He's never sure whether it's your thigh or toe that hurts until you point it out to him. This character was gradually abbreviated, by resting the kneecap 𝓻 on the foot 止, and was written in final form 足 . It is pronounced ASHI, which means **leg** or **foot**.

足 立 ADACHI, Foot-Stand, is a family

name. This should be pronounced ASHI-DACHI, of course, but since this is very difficult to say, it has been shortened to ADACHI. 足 立 區 ADACHI-KU, is Adachi Ward. In this ward also there is a Vehicle Registration Bureau, so you will see 足 立, or its abbreviation 足, on many license plates in Tokyo.

The picture of a foot 止 written with a straight line over it 正, meaning keep your foot on the straight and narrow, is the character for **correct** or **righteous** or **upright** or **legitimate**. It is usually pronounced TADASHII if used alone, and SEI or SHŌ in compounds. You will see 正 sometimes stamped on price tags to let you know the price is right.

The Japanese prefer words which denote exemplary character for their personal names, and 正 is one of their favorites. This character when used in proper names is usually pronounced TADA, MASA or SHŌ, and can appear in either first names or last:

正 子	MASAKO	Little-Righteous, a girl's name.
正 信	TADANOBU	Righteous-Trustworthy, a boy's name.

正力 SHŌRIKI Righteous-Power, a family name. This is the name of one of Japan's most versatile leaders, SHŌRIKI MATSU-TARO, founder of the Yomiuri business empire.

大正 TAISHŌ Great-Righteousness. This is the name of a large pharmaceutical manufacturer. It is also the name of the Japanese historical period between the Meiji period and the current Showa period.

A picture of a heart ♥ meant **heart**. The Chinese first wrote it 〔心〕, and finally 心. It is pronounced KOKORO by itself and SHIN in compounds. In Japanese, 心 means about the same as it does in English: not only is it one of the most important organs in the body but it is the center of the spirit and emotions as well. Some examples are:

小 心 SHOSHIN — small-heart. This means faint-heartedness, timidity, cautiousness.

心 付 KOKOROZUKE — put-up-against-heart. This is a tip, referring to either advice or a gratuity.

心 中 SHINJŪ — heart-inside. This means a double suicide.

When the sun 日 rises 立 the world awakens and the sound of life begins. The Chinese put these two characters together to form the character for **sound**. The new character is written 音. This is pronounced OTO when used by itself and ON or IN in compounds. An 足 音 ASHIOTO, foot-sound, is a footstep. A 母 音 BOIN, mother-sound, is a vowel, and a 子 音 SHIIN, child-sound, is a consonant.

Two hands ⺺ held over the heart 心 to temper

the excitement means **in a hurry, sudden, urgent, emergency.** The hands were written 〵/ and ⼹ and the final character became 㣇. Used by itself it is pronounced ISOGU. In compounds it is pronounced KYŪ.

The sound 音 of the heart 心 means the **mind.** This character is written 意, and is pronounced I. It means **mind,** with the connotation spirit, feelings, intentions, thoughts.

The next few characters have their origin in pictures of the sense organs, an eye was drawn first as it looked ⟨o⟩, then it was stood on end ⊖ and squared off to final form 目. It is pronounced ME, and means **eye.** This is the ME in CHŌME. No. 5 CHŌME is written 五 丁 目. 目白 White-Eyes, is a residential district in Tokyo.

The character for **hat** is a man measuring a piece of cloth 冒 to be used to shield the eyes 目 from the sun 日. The final character is put together like this 帽, pronounced BŌ. Hats in general are called 帽子 BŌSHI, little-hat. 學帽 GAKUBŌ, learning-hat, is a student's cap.

The man measuring cloth 冂 is also a character, although it is very seldom used alone. It does, however, appear in a number of other characters, to all of which it brings the meaning "cloth."

For the verb **to see**, the eye 目 is set atop a man 人. Man 人 changes shape and shrinks to ノL, and the final character is written 見. This is pronounced MIRU. A 見本 MIHON, seeing-the-original, is a sample.

A picture of an ear, lobe and all, 𝄀 formed the character for **ear**. It was first drawn 耳, and finally 耳. This is pronounced MIMI.

A hand ripping off an ear 取, in the manner one treated his enemies in former times, means **take**. When the two pictographs hand ㇗ and ear 耳 are combined in **take**, they both change shape slightly to form the final character 取. This is pronounced TORU.

The character for **teeth** 歯, like those for all the other parts of the face, was drawn about as it looked 歯. The final form of this character is 歯, although in modern times it is sometimes abbreviated further to 齒. In either form it is pronounced HA.

The character for **hair** is taken from a picture of a mandarin's wispy beard 毛. It was originally drawn 毛, and finally 毛. This is pronounced KE by itself and MO in compounds. It means both **human hair** and **animal fur.**

There are several views of noses. The front view of a nose 自, drawn as 畠 and finally as 鼻, means **nose.** This is pronounced HANA.

The Chinese point to their nose when referring to the self, while Westerners point to their chest. The character for nose 鼻, with the nostrils removed 自, became the character for **self.** This is pronounced JI.

The character for **self** 自 combined with the character for **wings** 羽 means fly-on-your-own-wings, or **learn.** At first the Chinese drew the character 習, but so often the two middle lines in 自 blurred together when writing it this way that they decided to drop one stroke, and finally chose to write it 習. This is pronounced NARAU by itself, and

SHŪ in compounds. Apprentice workers often wear. an arm band on which is written 見習 MI- NARAI, look-learn, meaning an apprentice or an on- the-job trainee.

A side view of the nose 厶, written 厶, was also used to indicate the **self** or **private**. This picto- graph, however, cannot be used alone but must be combined with other pictographs to form a character. One example of such a combination: a line | split in two became 八, and this pictograph means **split** or **divide**; combining the pictographs for **private** 厶 and **divide** 八 forms the character 公 KŌ, private- divided, meaning **not private**, therefore **public**.

Combining the character for public 公 with the character for tree 木 forms 松, meaning the pub- lic tree, the tree that's everywhere, the **pine**. It is pro- nounced MATSU. This is also a favorite for family and place names:

| 松田 MATSUDA | Pinetree-Paddy |
| 小松 KOMATSU | Small-Pine. This is the name of a leading Jap- anese machinery man- ufacturer, and also of a Ginza department store. |

松村 MATSUMURA Pine-village
松本 MATSUMOTO Pine-Origin
松下 MATSUSHITA Below-the-Pine. This is the name of the founder of the well known Matsushita Electric Company.

The nose meaning self or private 厶 is combined with a rice stalk tied for threshing 釆 to mean my private rice, or me. The rice stalk evolved from 釆 to 禾, then to 禾. Together with the nose it is written 私. This is pronounced WATAKUSHI or WATASHI by itself, where it means I or me, and SHI in compounds, where it means **private**. Anything, a school, for example, which is 私立 SHIRITSU, **private-standing,** is privately operated, as distinguished from State or City operated.

The rice stalk 禾 is also used as a building-block in several other characters. When added to a mouth 口 it means fat and happy, **peaceful** or **placid** or **tranquil** or **harmonious**. It is pronounced WA. The characters for the name of the Kyowa Bank, a well-known financial institution in Japan, are 協和 cooperate-in-harmony. The characters for Daiwa, another prominent bank, are 大 和, great-harmony.

大 和 is also, for some obscure reason, sometimes pronounced YAMATO, which is now the name of several towns in Japan but was once the name of Japan itself. 和 also appears in the name of a large department store on the main corner of the Ginza, the 和 光 WAKŌ, rays-of-harmony.

The rice stalk 禾 being inspected by the tax collector, who is big brother 儿 with horns 兒 means **tax.** The character for **big brother** is written 兄, and pronounced, with the addition of the appropriate kana, O-NIISAN. **Tax** is written 税, and pronounced ZEI. The 税 ZEI will of course be seen on all the "No Tax" signs in the tourist arcades, and will also be in the return address on any mail you get from the Tax Office.

The sayings 言 of big brother with horns 兒 is a **theory** or **opinion** or **story.** The completed character is written 説 and pronounced SETSU. A 小 説 SHŌSETSU, small-story, is a novel. A 説 明 SETSUMEI, theory-clear, is an explanation, and a 説 明 書 SETSUMEISHO, explanation-write, is the direction sheet which tells you how to use the products you have bought.

A crossroad 北 was written originally 北, and is now abbreviated in final form to 行. It means **go**. By itself it is pronounced IKU and in compounds KŌ. A 急 行 KYŪKŌ, hurry-go, is an express. This sign appears on all express trains.

The crossroads 行 widened slightly 彳 亍 with plenty of earth 圭 added, forms the character for avenue 街. This is pronounced GAI or KAI, whichever is most euphonious. Many of the major streets in Tokyo were called 街 until they were renamed DŌRI for the 1964 Olympics.

When the crossroads 行, meaning "to go", is combined with other pictographs to form new characters, just one side of the street is used 彳. Combined with temple 寺, it forms the new character 待. The temple was the community center in the olden days in China, so the character "go-to-the-temple" came to mean "wait for me at the temple", then simply **wait**. It is pronounced MATSU by itself and TAI in compounds.

The swirling form of whirlpool movement ⊙ meant **go around in circles.** The Chinese squared this picture off to 回 . This is pronounced MAWASU or MAWARU, the transitive and intransitive verb forms, when used by itself, and KAI in compounds. It means to **rotate, revolve, to go around,** or **circulate.** 二 回 NIKAI, two-rotations, means two times, second round, or second inning, depending on the context.

The next few characters were drawn from modes of locomotion.

A car or cart 車 was first drawn 車 then 車 . In final form the Chinese wrote it 車 . By itself it is pronounced KURUMA, and means **car** or **cart.** In compounds it is pronounced SHA, and brings to the compound the meaning wheeled-vehicle, of any type: an automobile, a bicycle, a rickshaw. The English word rickshaw, by the way, was borrowed from the Japanese word 人力車 JINRIKISHA, man-powered-vehicle. A 車体 SHATAI, car-body, is a car body or chassis, and a 車税 SHAZEI, car-tax, is a car tax.

A car 車 placed under a carport or lean-to 广 means **garage,** or more basically, **storage shed.** The completed character is written 庫 and pronounced KO. It cannot be used by itself, but needs another character or two preceding it to tell what kind of shed it is. 車庫 SHAKO, car-shed, is the proper word for garage.

A car 車 with an iron bumper mounted on it 軍 meant originally armored car or armored troops. It was written in final form 軍 and pronounced GUN. It later came to signify the entire army, not just the armored troops. With the Japanese abbreviation for America, 米 BEI, it means the American Army, 米軍 BEIGUN. A 軍人 GUNJIN is a military man, and 軍 GUN alone means **military**.

Used as a building-block for other characters, 軍 retains more the meaning of armored car than army. Combined with the pictograph which means **advance, proceed, go forward**, it forms the character for **transport, carry**. The pictograph for **advance** is itself composed of the abbreviated pictograph for go 彳 and the pictograph for foot, 止, first written 辵 then 辵, and finally 辶. The completed character for **transport** or **carry** is 運. By itself it is pronounced HAKOBU, and in compounds UN. This character, advancing-with-an-armored-car, also means **fate** or **destiny** or **luck**.

The pictograph for **advance** 辶 must be combined with other pictographs to form characters; it can never stand alone. It always brings to the new character the meaning **forward motion.** Another pictograph which can never stand alone is 关, a picture of a road ⚍ with a barrier or road-block set up across it 关. This pictograph is now written 关, and means **barrier,** a meaning which it brings to the characters it forms. Sending the **advance** pictograph 辶 around the **barrier** 关 forms the character for **send** 送. This is pronounced OKURU by itself and SŌ in compounds. The word 運送 UNSŌ, carry-send, means **transportation** or **moving.** These two characters, 運 and 送, appear on almost every truck used by freight or moving companies, and are generally used also in the names of these companies. The 石田運送 ISHIDA UNSŌ would be the Ishida Moving Co.

A man weighed down with a heavy pack on his back 重 means **heavy.** The Chinese first drew his picture 重 then 重, and finally 重. By itself this is pronounced OMOI, and in compounds JŪ. It means heavy in weight or heavy in burden. A 重税 JŪZEI is a heavy tax. 重大 JŪDAI, heavy-big means serious, grave. 体重 TAIJŪ, body-heaviness, means weight.

Power 力 applied to heaviness 重 forms 動, the character for **move**. By itself it is pronounced UGOKU, and in compounds DŌ. Some common applications:

自動車 JIDŌSHA self-move-car. This is an automobile. 車 is the generic category, including in it all types of wheeled-vehicles. 自動車 is an automobile specifically. All automobiles can be called KURUMA but not all KURUMA can be called automobiles. In speech the Japanese refer to automobiles as KURUMA or JIDŌSHA with about

運 動 UNDŌ carry-move. This means movement. This word generally refers to physical exercise, although it also refers to political movements. equal frequency.

Adding man 亻 to move 動 means **work** 働. By itself this character is pronounced HATARAKU, and in compounds DŌ.

The next few characters deal basically with money. Like most all the other early civilizations, the Chinese started out with shells for money, so these money characters are all built around the character for shell.

A **shell** itself ⟨⟩ was first written 貝 and finally 貝. This may seem similar to the character for **see** 見, but you can tell the difference by the bottom part, which is a man ノL in **see**, and a tail ノ 丶 in **shell**. 貝 is pronounced KAI and refers to any type of seashell.

A **shell** 貝 and a net ▨, abbreviated ⊏⊐, combined form the character 買, which refers to gathering things, or buying. The meaning of 買 is **to buy.** By itself it is pronounced KAU, and in compounds BAI.

The character for buy 買 placed under the character for coming out 出, abbreviated 士, forms the character 賣, **to sell.** This is pronounced URU by itself and BAI in compounds. 賣買 BAIBAI, buy-sell, means business or trade.

To sell 賣 speaking 言 means **to read.** The new character, 讀 is pronounced YOMU by itself and DOKU in compounds. One of Tokyo's leading newspapers is called the 讀賣 YOMIURI, Sold-Reading.

The seashell 貝, here also referring to money, combined with the radical for mouth 口, here referring to a man open-mouthed and talking, forms the character 員, meaning man-who-speaks-of-money. This now refers to a **store-clerk,** an **employee,** or a **staff member** of an organization. It is pronounced IN. This character cannot be used by itself, but must be preceded by one or two other characters which tell what kind of clerk or employee the person is. A 工 員 KŌIN, build-employee, is a factory hand.

A clerk 員 backed up against a coin ◯ means **Yen.** The coin is squared to ☐ but the clerk retains his shape. The new character is written 圓 , pronounced, of course, YEN. This is the old, respected form for Yen, used on bank checks, documents and receipts, and wherever else tradition, accuracy and beauty are important. It takes too long to write for modern business, however, so a new, simplified character was developed. Its shape must have been taken from a bank-teller's cage 凹 , for the final form is 円 . This is also pronounced YEN. It is the popular version, used beginning several years ago on money, in stores and throughout business generally, except on formal documents and papers where the old style is still retained.

The next few characters deal with gates. A **gate** itself is written 門 . This is pronounced MON, and refers to any kind of gate; the character that precedes it tells what kind of gate it is. JIGOKU-MON is Gate of Hell, RASHŌ-MON is Rasho's Gate, SUIMON 水 門 is sluice-gate, SANMON 山 門 is mountain-gate, now used to mean a gate to a Bhuddist temple. NYŪMON 入 門 , entrance-gate, is used in book titles to mean "...Primer" or "Elementary.....", and MON 門 alone is gate in general.

An ear 耳 at a gate 門 forms the character for **hear** 聞. This character is also used for **ask**. It is pronounced KIKU by itself, where it can mean either **hear** or **ask,** and BUN in compounds.

A mouth ☐ at the gate 門 forms another character for **ask** 問, although this one more in the sense of **question** or **interrogate.** This is pronounced TOU by itself, and MON in compounds. KIKU is the popular word for ask; TOU connotes more an inquiry, a petition.

The sun 日 shining between the gate doors 間 means **between,** or **time between** or **space between.** By itself it is pronounced AIDA and in compounds either KAN or MA. Some examples of its application are:

時 間 JIKAN   time-between. This is the popular word for time.

一 時 間 ICHIJIKAN one-hour-between. One hour.

二 時 間 NIJIKAN two-hours-between.

中 間 CHŪKAN — Two hours. middle-between. Middle, midway.

日 本 間 NIHONMA — Japan-between. Here the MA refers to space between, and means the space between the walls, a room. A NIHONMA is a Japanese-style room.

A gate 門 placed over a road-barrier 关 forms 関 meaning **barrier**. Whereas the pictograph for barrier 关 cannot be used alone to mean barrier, as we explained on page **80** , this character 関 can. By itself 関 is pronounced SEKI, and in compounds KAN. A few hundred years ago, during Japan's feudal period, a barrier of this type was set up dividing Western Japan from Eastern, and no one could pass unless they had the password. Eastern Japan was called KANTŌ 関 東 East-of-the-Barrier, and Western Japan was called KANSAI 関 西 , West-of-the-Barrier. The character for **west** is introduced on page **91**. KANTŌ is of course now used to describe Tokyo and its few surrounding prefectures, and KANSAI is used to mean the Kyoto-Osaka-Kobe district. Pronounced SEKI it is sometimes used as a family name. Some other applications are:

大 関 ŌZEKI   big-barrier. This is the second highest rank a sumo wrestler can hold.

税 関 ZEIKAN   tax-barrier. This is the Customs House or Customs.

Two hands removing the bar ψ丫 that locked the gate 門 means **to open**. The hands and the bar are written in final form 开 , and the completed character is 開 . This is pronounced AKERU or HIRAKU by itself and KAI in compounds.

A gate 門 with the cross-bar securely in place and braced 才 , written 閉 , means **to close**. This is pronounced TOJIRU by itself and HEI in compounds.

To indicate the meaning **door,** the Chinese used a half of a gate 昌 . This alone was out of balance, so they curved the vertical line and raised the top line into a cap 戸 . This is still æsthetically not attractive, but it was the best they could do with half a gate. It is pronounced TO. It is sometimes used in family names: 戸 田 TODA, Door-to-the-Paddy, and 戸 山 TOYAMA, Door-to-the-Mountain.

The next few dozen characters have to do with animals. Some of these characters consist of the abstract shape of the animal alone, these usually meaning the animal itself, and others consist of these abstract shapes plus other radicals, indicating a more involved meaning.

The first is horse 🐎. As in the well-known Chinese horse paintings, the horse was drawn as mainly mane and legs 馬, and finally in the most efficient way as 馬. This character means **horse**. It is pronounced UMA by itself and BA in compounds. A 馬 車 BASHA, horse-car, is a carriage; a 木 馬 MOKUBA, wood-horse, is a wooden horse, referring to either the merry-go-round or Trojan type; 一 馬 力 ICHIBARIKI, one-horse-power, is one horsepower; and 馬 肉 BANIKU is horsemeat.

The character for station, now mainly referring to a railroad station but in the olden days referring to horse or stagecoach stations, is formed from a picture of a man wearing a hachimaki, the Japanese headband, leaning on his shovel 𠘧 standing beside a horse 馬. The man and his shovel were originally written 𠘧, and finally 尺. The completed character is 駅, pronounced EKI. It appears on 東京駅 TŌKYŌ-EKI, 品川駅 SHINAGAWAEKI, and all the other stations in Japan.

A post-man 人 standing by his horse, pictured this time in rear view 𣆙, ready to mount 𠆢 and gallop down the post-road with the mail, means **mail.** The Chinese first wrote the horse 页 and finally 更. The completed character is written 便. From this picture the following meanings are also taken: an **airplane flight,** a **ship departure, convenience in general,** and **feces.** 便 is pronounced BEN or BIN. This character will be seen on all mail boxes and post offices in Japan. Japan Air Lines 二 便 NI-BIN is JAL Flight Two. BENJO, the JO for which is introduced on page 113, is the vernacular for lavatory. This word is polite enough for ordinary conversation —although the ladies generally avoid using it — and it is used on the doors of many public rest rooms. A more dignified synonym for BENJO, ·however, is

O-TEARAI, honorable-hand-washing-place.

The Chinese picture for a bird was ![bird], later shortened to ![bird], and finally 鳥. This became the character for **bird**. It is pronounced TORI, and refers to any kind of bird. The four dots at the bottom of this character represent the bird's tail feathers, while the four dots at the bottom of the horse 馬, although they are drawn in the same way, represent the horse's legs.

A bird 鳥 flying over a mountain 山 became the character for **island**. This was first written ![island], but later it was tightened up by removing the tail feathers and raising the mountain in its place 島. This is pronounced SHIMA by itself and TO in compounds. Like the other words of nature, SHIMA is a favorite choice for family names:

島	SHIMA	Island
下 島	SHIMOJIMA	Lower-Island
中 島	NAKAJIMA	Middle-Island
川 島	KAWASHIMA	River-Island
島 田	SHIMADA	Island-Paddy
松 島	MATSUSHIMA	Pine-Island

A bird returning to its nest 🐦 ; as it does at dusk when the sun is in the west means **west.** The Chinese first wrote this 西 and finally 西 . It is pronounced NISHI by itself and SEI or SAI in compounds. We have already seen that 関 西 KANSAI, west-of-the-barrier, is the Osaka-Kobe District. 西 日 本 NISHI-NIHON is Far-West Japan. Many firms in that part of the country have taken this as their name. Many railroad stations, of course, have a 西 口 NISHIGUCHI, west-entrance. 西 is also used in family names:

西	山	NISHIYAMA	West-Mountain
西	林	NISHIBAYASHI	West-Woods
中	西	NAKANISHI	Mid-West

The Chinese had another picture of a bird, this one a short-tailed bird 🐦 , which they wrote first 隹 then 隹 and finally 隹 . This bird cannot appear alone. It must be used with other pictographs to form characters, to which, of course, it brings the meaning **bird.** The Chinese combined this **bird** 隹 with the pictographs for **sun** or **day** 日 and **wings** 羽 to form the character 曜 YŌ, sun-flying-by-on-bird's-wings, meaning **days of the week.**

The Japanese names of the days of the week are

taken from the names of the seven basic nature symbols: sun, moon, fire, water, wood, metal, and earth. These names are followed by 曜 meaning **days of the week,** and finally, for emphasis, by **day** 日 .

日 曜 日 NICHIYŌBI	Sun-day. Sunday.
月 曜 日 GETSUYŌBI	Moon-day. Monday.
水 曜 日 SUIYŌBI	Water-day. Wednesday.
木 曜 日 MOKUYŌBI	Wood-day. Thursday.
土 曜 日 DOYŌBI	Earth-day. Saturday.

There are several characters meaning **to arrive.** One is derived from a picture of a bird diving from the sky down to the ground 𝕎 . The Chinese first drew this bird 𝕎 , then 至 , and in final form 至 . It is pronounced ITARU. Although still popular in China as a word for **arrive,** this character is now used in Japan mainly on road signs, where it means "to...," literally "road-for-arriving-at....." The sign 至 東 京 ITARU TOKYO means "this way to Tokyo."

Arriving 至 under a roof ∧ forms the character for **room** 室. This is pronounced SHITSU, and is generally preceded by one or two other characters defining what type of room it is. A 和 室 WA-

SHITSU Japan-room, is a Japanese style room. The old name for Japan was 大和, and the abbreviation of this, 和 WA, is still used to refer to things Japanese.

A picture of a man with a hachimaki, a headband, wrapped around his head 戸 is the pictograph for tradesman. We saw him leaning on his shovel in the character for station 尺. The tradesmen in Japan, even now, tie a cloth or towel around their head to show they are at work. Combining 戸 with the character for arrive 至 forms 屋, which signifies arriving at the tradesman's. This has come now to mean simply a **tradesman** or **tradesman's shop.** It is pronounced YA. When it refers to the tradesman himself, rather than to his shop, the term for mister, SAN, is generally added after YA.

肉 屋 NIKUYA   meat-man or meat-shop. To be polite you call the butcher a NIKUYA-SAN rather than simply a NIKUYA.

魚 屋 SAKANAYA fish-monger or fish shop. Many department stores also use 屋 in their name:

白木屋 SHIROKIYA White-Tree-Shop. This store is located on one corner of the Nihonbashi Intersection.

松坂屋 MATSUZAKAYA Pine-Hill-Shop. This is located on the Ginza.

Another word for shop is 店. The character for this word is formed from a picture of a long-nosed clerk standing behind a counter 占 set up under a lean-to 广. It is pronounced MISE by itself and TEN in compounds. Some examples of its use are:

書店 SHOTEN writings-shop. This is a book store.

本店 HONTEN origin-shop, the main store. Big department stores and other chains generally have a 本店 HONTEN, a main store, and 支店 SHITEN, branch stores.

賣店 BAITEN sales-shop. This is a stall or portable shop set up to sell cigarettes, candy and sundries at railroad stations, ballgames, parks, etcetera.

A bird trying to fly straight up, toward heaven, but being blocked from ever reaching there 丕 , means negative: **dis-, un-, mis-**. The final written form is 不 ,pronounced FU. Some applications are:

不便 FUBEN In-convenient.

不明 FUMEI Un-clear. This means indistinct, unknown.

不二家 FUJIYA Not-two-houses. This defies meaningful translation, but it is the name of a very popular restaurant chain with stores Japan-wide.

The character for **cow** is a front-view picture of his face 牛 . The first abstraction was 牛 , then it was reduced to 牛 . Finally, one horn was removed to form the current writing 牛 . This means **cow** or **bull** or **ox,** and is pronounced USHI by itself and GYŪ in compounds. A 子牛 KO-USHI, is a calf; 牛肉 GYŪNIKU, cow-meat, is beef.

A cow 🐂 combined with an elephant 🐘 means **things.** The cow, as shown in the preceding paragraph, was abstracted to 牛 . The elephant was abstracted to trunk and tusks 勿 . The final form of this new character is 物 pronounced MONO by itself and BUTSU in compounds. It refers to **things** or **articles** in general:

物 語 MONOGATARI things-tell. This means story or tales, as in Genji Monogatari —The Tales of Genji.

名 物 MEIBUTSU name-article. This means a famous product or a souvenir. Many Japanese towns and most resorts have their 名 物 MEIBUTSU, or special native product, which they try to sell you as a souvenir.

賣 物 URIMONO sell-thing. This means "for sale."

買 物 KAIMONO buy-things. This means "go shopping."

A bull 牛 in the temple 寺 means **special**, something out of the ordinary. The character is written 特, and pronounced TOKU. It is used wherever the word **special** applies: special service, special express, special program, and especially. A 特急 TOKKYŪ (TOKUKYŪ abbreviated) is a special express. This is even faster than a 急行 KYŪKŌ.

A hand 爪 holding a child 子 against a breast 乚 forms **milk**. This is written 乳, and pronounced NYŪ. Every milk bottle in Japan has 牛乳 GYŪNYŪ written somewhere on it.

A **sheep** is also a front-view picture of its head 𦍋. The first abstraction was 羊, and the final form 羊. It means **sheep** or **ram**. By itself it is pronounced HITSUJI and in compounds YŌ. 羊毛 YŌMŌ, sheep-hair, means wool.

For the Chinese, sheep 羊 were in the land beyond the water 水 so a character showing sheep beyond the water 水羊 was made to mean **ocean**. Since 水 is written 氵 when used as a building-block, the final form of **ocean** is 洋. It is pronounced YŌ. Some examples are:

西洋 SEIYŌ	West-Ocean. This refers to the Western countries, the Occident.
西洋人 SEIYŌJIN	West-Ocean-Man. This is a Westerner, an Occidental.
東洋人 TŌYŌJIN	East-Ocean-Man. This is an Easterner, an Oriental.
大西洋 TAISEIYŌ	Great-West-Ocean. This is the Atlantic Ocean.
洋品店 YŌHINTEN	ocean-goods-store. Here 洋 is an abbreviation of 西洋 SEIYŌ, Occident. A 洋品店 therefore, is a shop which sells western-style products.
洋間 YŌMA	western-room. Here again 洋 YŌ is the abbreviation of Occidental. This means a west-

ern-style room, as distinguished from a 日本間 NIHONMA, or a 和室 WASHITSU, Japanese-style room. Most of the major hotels in Japan have both 洋間 YŌMA and 日本間 NIHONMA. The Japanese inns have 日本間 NIHONMA only.

洋菓子 YŌGASHI western-sweets. 菓子 alone is the generic term for sweets, including cake, cookies, rice-cakes (sembei), chocolates, etc. 洋菓子 refers to Western-style cakes. 和菓子 WAGASHI refers to the Japanese-style cakes, made mostly from sweet bean-paste.

The Chinese combined the radical for water 氵 with the radical for every 毎 to form the character for **sea** 海. This is pronounced UMI by itself and KAI in compounds. The 日 本 海 NIHONKAI is the Japan Sea. 海 上 KAIJŌ, on-the-sea, means maritime. These two characters written in reverse order, 上 海 by the way, form the name of the city of Shanghai.

A big 大 sheep 羊, stacked like this 美 means **beautiful.** It is compressed and written 美 in final form. By itself it is pronounced UTSUKUSHII, and in compounds BI. A 美 人 BIJIN, beautiful-person, is a beautiful girl.

A picture of a pig was drawn successively , , and finally 豕. To form the written character for **pig,** the pictograph for meat 月 is added, 豚. This is pronounced BUTA when used alone and TON in compounds. TON-KATSU, a popular local dish, is pork cutlet. KATSU is the closest the Japanese can get to the pronounciation of cutlet. On menus KATSU will be written in kana and the TON is 豚.

The original pig 豕 under a roof 宀, squared off to 家 means **house.** At first it referred to pig sties only, but now it is used for any type of house. It is pronounced IE by itself and KA in compounds.

The Chinese put a woman 女 under a roof 宀 and made **peace** 安. This character also has the meaning **inexpensive, cheap.** It is pronounced YASUI by itself and AN in compounds. A 安物 YASU-MONO, cheap-thing, is an inferior article: a 安賣 YASUURI, cheap-sell, is a rummage sale.

A **fish** 🐟 was pictured first as 魚 then 魚, and finally 魚. This is pronounced SAKANA, and refers to any kind of fish.

The character for **thread** is drawn from a silk-worm's cocoon 8. The Chinese first wrote it 糸, and finally 糸. It is pronounced ITO. This character originally referred to silk thread only, but now it means any kind of thread. The type of thread is usually indicated by a suffix, as for example 毛糸, KEI-TO, hair-thread, meaning woolen yarn.

Water flowing from a natural spring is usually pure and clear. To form the character for **natural spring** the Chinese took the radicals for water 水 and white 白, and put them together like this 泉. This character is pronounced IZUMI by itself and SEN in compound.

A favorite Japanese diversion is a few days vacation at a hot spring resort. To write the word "hot spring," add the character for **warm** (because if the hot spring were really hot you couldn't bathe in it) to the character for spring 泉

The character for **warm** is a picture of the sun 日 warming water ; on a plate 皿. The pictograph for **plate**, which when written by itself is the character for **plate**, pronounced SARA, was first written 皿 and finally 皿. The character for **warm** is written in final form 温, and is pronounced ON.

A hot spring, therefore, is an 温泉 ONSEN. The mark ♨ which you see at all the 温泉, is not a character, just a symbol of a hot spring.

Like other words of nature, 泉 is used in personal names:

小 泉　KOIZUMI　Small-Spring
大 泉　ŌIZUMI　　Big-Spring
泉 屋　IZUMIYA　House-of-Izumi. This is the

name of a prominent confectionary in Tokyo owned by a Mrs. Izumi.

A 体 温 計 TAIONKEI, body-warmth-measure, is a clinical thermometer. An 温 室 ONSHITSU, warm-room, is a green house or hot house.

Adding thread or line 糸 to spring 泉 forms 線, which indicates the line the falling water forms. This character means **line,** and is used to designate a railroad line, lines on a sheet of paper, a line or beam of light; in short, anything we call a line in English. It is pronounced SEN.

山 手 線 YAMATE-SEN The Yamate Line, Mountain-Hand-Line, the loop line which circles Tokyo.

中 央 線 CHUŌ-SEN The Chuo Line, Central-Line, the rail line running from Tokyo west.

光 線 KŌSEN ray-line. Light beams.

Icicles hanging from roof eaves 氷 the Chinese

used to symbolize **winter**. They drew this character first 冬 , and finally 冬 . This is pronounced FUYU.

The "winter" 冬 of a thread 糸 means the **end**. The final character is written 終 and pronounced OWARU or OWARI. This character will flash as the last scene on movie and TV screens, and end most books in Japanese.

A dog was pictured first as 犬 , then 犬 and finally very abstractedly as 犬 . This is the character for **dog**, and is pronounced INU. A 小 犬 KOINU, is a puppy, and an 犬 小 屋 INUGOYA, dog-small-house, is a doghouse.

Four mouths 吅 around a dog 犬 means **plate** or **vessel**. The final form is 器 , with the dog's ear missing. It is pronounced KI. This character was formed when dog meat was a delicacy, and referred to the vessels and utensils it took to make and eat a meal. In modern usage it has been extended somewhat to include other types of vessels and utensils. Some types of pottery use this character, as do some types of weapons. 器 is usually prefixed by another character which tells the type of vessel or utensil referred to. 土器 DOKI, earth-vessel, is earthenware.

A wild beast's footprint 🐾 is now the character for **number**. This may be how the ancients learned to count. In olden days a beast was used as a guard at night, so this character is also used to mean **guard**. In either case it is pronounced BAN. The final written form is 番. Some examples of its application are:

一 番 ICHIBAN   one-number. This means number one, and also means "the best."

十 番 JŪBAN   ten-number. This means number ten.

番 人 BANNIN   guard-man. This is the watchman.

門 番 MONBAN   gate-guard. This is the gate-keeper.

番 is also the BAN in KŌBAN, which is the little street-corner police box seen everywhere in Japan.

While BAN is the generic term for number, another character is used as the prefix indicating an ordinal number. This prefix translates as **-irst, -ond, -rd, -th,** depending on which number follows it. The character for this word represents some bamboo slats tied with strings into a crude abacus which was used as a primitive counting machine. The slats and string tied together looked like this 畕 . The Chinese drew them first 弗 , then 弗 , and finally 弟 . To show that they were made of bamboo, the Chinese added the character for bamboo at the top.

The character for **bamboo** was a picture of the leaves 竹竹 drawn just as they are still pictured on Oriental scrolls and paintings, squared off to 竹 for ease in writing. The finished character looked like this 第 . It is pronounced DAI. Bamboo alone 竹 is pronounced TAKE.

第 —— DAIICHI First. Besides being a number, this is also a very popular company name, signifying "foremost" as it does. There is the Daiichi Hotel, the Daiichi Insurance Company, and many, many others.

第 二 DAINI Second.

One hundred is one —— bag of rice 白 which weighs one hundred pounds. The bag of rice is represented by a grain of rice 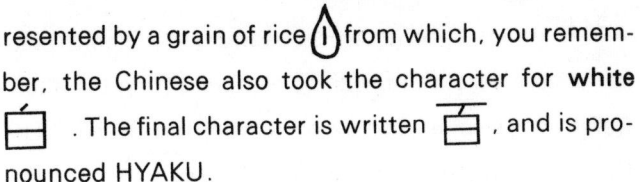 from which, you remember, the Chinese also took the character for **white** 白 . The final character is written 百 , and is pronounced HYAKU.

One hundred 百 men 人 under a roof ⌒ means **hotel**. This character is written 宿 , and is pronounced YADO by itself and SHUKU in compounds. A 宿屋 YADOYA, hotel-tradesman's, is a hotel. A 下宿 GESHUKU, lower-hotel, is a boardinghouse. 宿 is also used in place names. 三宿 MISHUKU, is a residential section of Tokyo.

The character for **one thousand** is combined from ten 十 and men 人 . Superimposing one atop the other, the Chinese first wrote it 仟 , then squared it into 千 . It is generally pronounced SEN by itself and CHI in compounds. 千 is also sometimes used in names. As the abbreviation for Chiba Prefecture, it appears on the license plates of autos registered in Chiba.

The character for **ten thousand** the Chinese borrowed from the ancient Indian religious symbol

卍 , which meant ten thousand gods. The Greeks borrowed it from the Indians also, and then the Third Reich in Germany borrowed it from the Greeks. The Germans wrote it backwards, however, 卐. The Chinese first wrote it like this 万 , and finally 万 . It is pronounced MAN. 一万 ICHIMAN, one-ten-thousand, is ten thousand; 十万 JŪMAN, ten-ten-thousand, is one hundred thousand.

The next group of characters take their form from weapons. These weapons are all the hand-held type, of course, since these were the only weapons the Chinese had to fight with in the days before they invented gunpowder.

A picture of a bow and arrow 弓 , means **pull**. The final form of this character is 引 . It is pronounced HIKU by itself and IN in compounds. This character is often written on the handle of one side of swinging doors. The handle on the other side has written on it the character for push. 引力 IN-RYOKU, pulling-power, means gravity.

An arrow by itself 矢 the Chinese drew first with full tip and feathers 矢 , then later squared it off to 矢 . This character means arrow, and is pronounced YA.

An arrow 矢 and a mouth ▢ combined forms 知, arrow-speaking, talking straight, which means **to know**. It is pronounced SHIRU by itself and CHI in compounds. Some examples of its use are:

知名　CHIMEI　known-name. This means well-known.

知人　CHIJIN　known-person. This is an acquaintance.

知事　CHIJI　know-things. This is a State or Prefectural Governor. Governor Azuma is 東知事 AZUMA CHIJI.

An arrow 矢 in the chest, the human chest, 匚, forms the character for **doctor** 医. (Pulling arrows out of wounded soldiers was after all one of the earliest practices of doctors everywhere.) It is pronounced I.

In Japan it is the system for doctors, even though they may be attached to the larger hospitals or universities, to have their own small clinic, usually with a few beds. These clinics are scattered throughout the city, so even in the most residential of sections you will see this lighted sign 矢 which marks the doctor's office.

矢 is the modern character for **doctor**, an abbreviation of the older one, still sometimes used, which is 醫 . The upper-lefthand segment of the old character is the arrow-in-the-chest which is the abbreviation of the whole. The upper-righthand pictograph 殳 is a hand holding a weapon or scalpel . The bottom pictograph 酉 is a jar containing alcohol , the disinfectant or the anesthetic, no one now knows which.

The jar containing alcohol 酉 , with the addition of the pictograph for water 氵 to show the jar is full, means **wine** or **liquor**, written in final form 酒 . It is pronounced SAKE by itself and SHU in compounds. This refers to liquor in general, but at the same time it is the character for **sake**, the Japanese rice-wine. Sake is sometimes called 日本酒 NIHONSHU also. 洋酒 YŌSHU refers to western liquors. Sometimes the E in SAKE is changed to A for euphony, as for example in 酒場 SAKABA, wine-place, meaning bar, and SAKAYA 酒屋 , wine-shop, meaning liquor store.

The English word "bar," pronounced BĀ in Japanese, has almost completely replaced 酒場 SAKABA in reference to bars which serve whiskey, so the sign 酒 場 is usually now seen only on traditional bars which serve sake only. There are no characters for BĀ, of course, and this is always written in kana.

酒 家 SHUKA, wine-house, is one Chinese word for restaurant, used to designate a Chinese restaurant which serves liquor. You will see this in the name and shop signs of many Chinese restaurants in Tokyo.

The Chinese first drew a knife showing just the blade 刀 . The final form for this was 刀 , the character for **knife** or **sword**. It is pronounced KATANA.

Combinining knife 刀 with the picture of a line divided /\ forms the character meaning **divide** or **cut into pieces** 分 . This is extended to mean **minute**, a division of the hour. It is pronounced WAKERU by itself and FUN or BUN, sometimes euphonically PUN, in compounds. Some examples are:

一 分 IPPUN one-minute. This would be normally be pronounced ICHI-

FUN, but this is awkward so the Japanese have decided to abbreviate it IPPUN. It means one minute.

五 分 GOFUN five-minutes.

十 分 JIPPUN ten-minutes. Pronounced this way, it means ten minutes. This should be pronounced JŪFUN, but this again is awkward, so the Japanese decided to use JIPPUN.

十 分 JŪBUN ten-parts. Pronounced this way, even though exactly the same characters as the word above are used, it means **enough**.

自 分 JIBUN self-part. This means myself, me.

When it appears as a radical in other characters, knife 刀 is written 刂. Combining this form of knife with a ripe rice stalk 禾 forms the character 利, cutting the rice. This is the equivalent of the English "cutting the pie," and means **profit**. It is pronounced RI. Some examples are:

利回 RIMAWARI profit-go-round. This is the yearly interest paid on stocks or bonds.

不利 FURI unprofitable.

利口 RIKŌ profit-mouth. This means clever, shrewd, smart.

The knife 刂 separating flesh from bones 𤴐 means **separate**. The skeleton was first written 𤴐, then 另, and finally 另. The completed character is 別. It is pronounced BETSU. It is both the verb **separate**, where it means separate in the sense of "to part from," and the adjective **separate**, "separate checks."

A hacksaw and a door 戸 together mean **place**. Hacksaw was written by the Chinese 斤, and placed beside the door 所. This word is **place** in the generic sense; it can be used wherever you can use the English word place. By itself it is pronounced TOKORO, and in compounds SHO or JO. A 便所 BENJO, convenient-place, is a lavatory.

The character for **place** meaning a specific place where activities go on is formed from ground 土

and sun 旦 and a picture of the flags the Chinese used to call the people together 㓁 . The flags were first written 㓁 and finally 勿 . The horizontal line below the sun is the horizon. The completed character is written 場, and pronounced BA or JŌ. Some applications are:

工 場 KŌBA build-place. This means factory.

工 場 KŌJŌ build-place. Used with the character 工 場 can be pronounced either BA or JŌ. In either case it means factory.

運 動 場 UNDŌJŌ exercise-place. This is a playground.

A hand 扌 and a hacksaw 斤 together form the character for **bend**. The meaning is also extended to **fold** or **crease** or **turn**. When 手 is used as a building-block, you remember, it is written 扌 . The final form of this character, then, is written 折 . It is pronounced ORU when used by itself and SETSU in compounds. The traffic signs all use this character when they say 左 折 SASETSU, left-turn, and 右

折 USETSU, right-turn.

The hacksaw 斤 sawing off some of the forward motion from the **advance** pictograph 辶 forms the character for **close by** or **near**. The final character is written 近, and is pronounced CHIKAI by itself and KIN in compounds. 近所 KINJO, near-place, means neighborhood. Almost all the movie theaters in Japan have somewhere in their theater a billboard over which is written 近日公開 KINJITSU KŌKAI, near-days public-opening, meaning "opening soon." 近東 KINTŌ is the Near East, referring to the countries at the east end of the Mediterranean Sea.

The character for **new** shows a tree 木 placed under stand 立 and beside the hacksaw 斤, signifying, with the oriental sense of destiny, that each new stand of timber will be cut. The completed character is 新. By itself it is pronounced ATARASHII, and in compounds SHIN. It means **new**. A 新聞 SHINBUN, new-hearings, is a newspaper. 新 is also popular in place names: 新宿区 SHIN-JUKU-KU, New-Hotel-Ward is a Ward in Tokyo.

Two hacksaws 斤斤 poised above a shell 貝 ready to dissect it to see what is inside means **character** or **nature** or **quality**. It also means **pawn**, where the meaning is derived from the concept of sawing money, represented by the shell, into little pieces, which is what most pawning leads to. It is pronounced SHITSU or SHICHI. 質 SHITSU alone means quality in the abstract; 品質 HINSHITSU, goods-quality, means quality of specific goods. A 質問 SHITSUMON, asking-the-nature, is a question. A 質屋 SHICHIYA is a pawn shop.

The Chinese felt that there are certain times, as in a war, when an ax 弋 can replace a man 人 They combined these two pictographs to write the character for **replace**. First they pictured ax as 弋 and finally as 弋 Then they added man 亻 and formed the final character 代. Used by itself it is pronounced KAWARU, and in compounds DAI or YO.

Its primary meaning is **replace**, but it is extended to mean any sort of **replacement**—generations of people which replace each other, eras or ages which replace each other, deputies or agents whose actions replace for yours, and the money which replaces the goods and services you receive from others. It is also used in proper names. Some common examples are:

代書屋 DAISHOYA replace-write-tradesman. This is a scribe, someone who will do your writing for you. There are still people in Japan who earn their living through this occupation. This has nothing to do with a literacy problem, however. The Japanese are quite meticulous about the visual impression their documents make, and pay the 代書屋 to render the contents in proper and attractive style.

タクシ代 TAXI DAI Taxi fare. The Japanese word for taxi is taxi, written in kana.

近代 KINDAI Near-era. This means modern times.

千代田 CHIYODA Field-of-a-thousand-generations. This is the name of the Tokyo ward which contains much of the downtown Tokyo area.

代々木 YOYOGI

Generations-and-generations-of-trees. When the same character is used twice in a row, Japanese ditto marks 々 replace the second character 代々木 is the name of a residential area in western Tokyo.

To replace 代 goods for money, which is represented by a shell 貝, is **to lend** or **rent**. The completed character is 貸, pronounced KASU or KASHI. Signs on many new office buildings advertise 貸室受付中 KASHISHITSU UKETSUKECHŪ, rent-rooms reception-middle, meaning Office For Rent —Applications Accepted.

An ax 弋 and a ruler 工 together 式 mean

method or **style.** It also means **ceremony.** 式 is pronounced SHIKI.

日本式 NIHONSHIKI

Japan-style. This refers to Japanese style, in houses, customs, way of thinking, furniture, or other matters.

アメリカ式 AMERIKASHIKI

America-style. This is the American way. America is written in kana.

洋式 YŌSHIKI foreign-style. This the Western way of doing things.

式場 SHIKIJŌ ceremony-hall. This sign will be posted at the entrance to halls where marriages, grand-openings, celebrations, and other great affairs are being held.

The character for **fire** is a picture of a flame 凶. The character was first written 凶 then 火, and finally 火. It is pronounced HI by itself and KA in compounds. 火曜日 KAYOBI, fire-day, is Tuesday. A 火事 KAJI, fire-affair, is a fire. This is what you yell when you want to spread a fire alarm. A 火山 KAZAN, fire-mountain, is a volcano.

The character for a **flame** itself was formed from two fires, one atop the other 炎. This is pronounced HONOO.

Fire 火 added to a lot of earth piled up 垚 atop a table 兀 forms the character 燒, which means **to bake** or **roast** or **burn.** This originated from the first experience in making pottery where you pile up shaped earth in an oven, add fire, and bake. It is pronounced YAKU or YAKERU. Some applications are:

夕燒 YŪYAKE   Burnt-evening. The sunset.

燒肉 YAKINIKU Roast-meat. This refers generally to meat cooked over an open fire or on a charcoal brazier as for example the Koreans and North Asians do. The sign

燒 肉 YAKINIKU appears on all the many Korean restaurants in Tokyo.

燒 場 YAKIBA burn-place. This a crematorium.

Fire 火 on the ground 土 blown by the prevailing wind from the west 西 means **smoke.** This character is put together like this 煙, and is pronounced EN.

Fire 火 set to tied and bundled rice stalks 禾 means **autumn,** written 秋 and pronounced AKI. 秋 田 AKITA, autumn-field, is the name of a prefecture in northern Japan. An 秋 田 犬 AKITA-INU, autumn-field-dog, is a well-known Japanese breed, formerly used for hunting and fighting. 秋 山 AKIYAMA, autumn-mountain, is a family name.

A fire set to a pile of cut and dried-out grass 㷀 means **nothing.** When the pictograph for fire is used as the bottom segment of a new character it changes shape from 火 to灬. The pile of grass is written 無 and the finished character 無. This is pronounced NAI or NASHI when used by itself, and MU in compounds.

It is used to indicate the negative side of anything. 無 線 MUSEN, no-wire, means wireless and a taxi with the sign 無 線 車 MUSENSHA, no-wire-car, is one with a radio-telephone. 無 口 MUKUCHI, no-mouth, means silent or taciturn.

The character for the color **black** 黒 looks like it might have been formed from fire,\\\field 田 and earth 土 . If this helps you to remember it, leave it at that. The Chinese, however, were actually thinking of a window 田 being blackened by the soot from a flame 炎 . When 炎 is combined with other pictographs to form a character, the lower fire changes shape, as we saw above, to ,\\\, and the upper fire changes to 火 and finally 土 , the new flame becoming therefore 赤 . The final character 黒 , incidentally, is still used in Chinese to mean "soot." 黒 is pronounced KUROI by itself and KOKU in compounds. 目 黒 MEGURO, Black-Eye, is a residential district in Tokyo. 黒 田 KURODA, Black-Field, is a family name.

The color **red** is a picture of hell—a fire 火 below the earth 土 . When the character for fire is used as a part of other characters it usually changes shape to ⼩, essentially four dots. In the character **red**, however, since the earth radical 土 is such a simple shape, the fire dots are written large 小 to give the character body 赤. It is pronounced AKA or AKAI when used by itself and SEKI in compounds. 赤坂 AKASAKA, Red-Hill, is the name of Tokyo's Night Club area. A 赤外線 SEKIGAISEN red-outside-line, is an infra-red ray.

The Chinese use the same character to mean both **blue** and **green**. The character is formed from a blue moon 月 seen rising up through green foliage 𡗗. The foliage is squared off to 𦥑, and then combined with moon 青. It is pronounced AO or AOI. 青山 AOYAMA, green-mountain, or blue-mountain, is a district in Tokyo. 青木 AOKI, green-wood or blue-wood, is a common family name.

The same leaves 𦥑 combined with mother 母 becomes the character for **poison** 毒, pronounced DOKU. 毒 will be written on all the bottles containing harmful poisons, and elsewhere where the skull and crossbones would be expected to appear.

The character for **color** itself, which is at the same time the character for **things erotic,** is a picture of a Peeping Tom on a roof looking through an open window 色 . The final form of the character is 色 , and is pronounced IRO. The use of this word in the first sense, where it means **color,** is rather straightforward: wherever you would use the word color in English you can substitute IRO. An examples of its use in the second sense is 色 目 IROME color-eyes, which means "make eyes at" or "ogle at."

A picture of a man bending over the edge of a cliff 厃 looking for his friend who has just toppled over and lies below 卩 forms the character for **dangerous** 危. This is pronounced ABUNAI by itself and KI in compounds. This character must by law appear written clearly on trucks and other vehicles carrying dangerous cargo. It is also posted in all other places where danger is a menace.

The next few characters involve man in different postures, each character taking its meaning from man and the posture he appears in.

The first is a man standing on his feet 人 beside another sitting down 匕 . The standing man you know already 人 ; the seated man was drawn like this 匕 The new character was written 化, meaning **to change from one form into another,** and pronounced KA or KE. Women's makeup is 化粧 KESHŌ, change-paint. The character for SHŌ is formed from the pictograph for rice 米 (which is what the Chinese first used for cosmetic powder) and the pictograph for earth or clay 土 stored under a shed 广. The character 粧 SHŌ means **to apply paint or powder to, to embellish.** Cosmetics are 化粧品 KESHŌHIN, make-up-things. This sign will appear on cosmetic shop-fronts and on cosmetic counters in department stores. The elegant term for lavatory is 化粧室 KESHŌSHITSU, makeup-room. This sign is used in all the better hotels and restaurants. 化學 KAGAKU, change-study, means chemistry. 化 is also used as a building-block in forming new characters, to each of which it brings the meaning of **changing from one form into another.**

The character for **flower** is one of these. The pictograph for plants 十十 is combined with the pictograph for changing-from-one-form-to-another 化 to form the character for flower 花 This is pronounced HANA by itself, and KA in compounds. A 花屋

HANAYA is a flower-shop or flower-shop operator. 花火 HANABI, fire-flowers, are fireworks. 活 花 IKEBANA, living-flowers, is the art of flower arranging. (活 is pronounced KATSU except in this compound where it is pronounced IKE.)

Two men seated back-to-back atop the world 𫝀 mean **North.** This character is written without the world 北, and is pronounced KITA by itself and HOKU in compounds. The 北海, pronounced HOKKAI, (HOKUKAI abbreviated) north-sea, is the North Sea. Hokkaido, the northernmost of Japan's four major islands, uses the two characters 北海 for the first two syllables of its name. The character for the last syllable, -**do,** has not been introduced yet.

Two men seated facing in the same direction 比 mean **compare.** The final form of this character is 比. It is pronounced KURABERU by itself and HI in compounds. A park in downtown Tokyo is called 日比谷 HIBIYA, Comparative-Sun-Valley.

An old man, cane in hand, with long hair flowing in the wind 長 means **long.** The Chinese first drew him 長, then 長, and finally in present form 長

This is pronounced NAGAI by itself and CHŌ in compounds. In addition to the meaning long, it also indicates the **top man** in a group or organization: the mayor, the president, the oldest son, the section chief, the railroad-station master, the straw boss, the Board Chairman. Some examples are:

駅長 EKICHŌ — Station-chief.
The rail road-station master.

支店長 SHITENCHŌ — Branch-shop-chief.
The Branch Manager.

工場長 KŌJŌCHŌ — Work-place-chief.
The Factory Manager.

長女 CHŌJO — Chief-girl.
The eldest daughter.

長男 CHŌNAN — Chief-boy.
The eldest son.

Two hunchbacks facing each other 亞 means **hunchback.** This character, written in final form 亞 also indicates the meaning "something less than first class" or "sub-". It is pronounced A. For some reason it was selected as the phonetic for the A in Asia.

Hunchback 亞 combined with heart 心 forms

the character for **bad** 惡 . This is pronounced WARUI by itself and AKU in compounds. 惡 口 WARUGUCHI, bad-mouth, means to malign or slander. 惡 化 AKKA (originally AKUKA) bad-change, means to worsen.

The character for **king** is composed of a line at the top ⎯ , symbolizing heaven, a line in the middle ⎯⎯ , symbolizing man, a line at the bottom ＿ , symbolizing earth, all held together by a vertical line │ symbolizing that which holds the world together, the **king** . The final form for this character is 王 , pronounced Ō. The three lines—heaven, man, and earth—will be familiar to students of flower arrangement who learn these lines and their relative positions as important symbols in flower arranging.

The SANNŌ 山 王 Hotel, well known to many of the American military people in Japan, is the King-of-the-Mountain Hotel. 京 王 KEIŌ, Capital-King, is the name of a department store, in Shinjuku. The 京 王 線 KEIŌSEN, Capital-King Line, is a railroad line running from Shinjuku west.

The character for king 王 with the addition of a jewel ○ , symbolizing the national treasure, drawn in beside it 玉 , means **jewel.** It is pronounced TAMA. It sometimes refers to round objects in general, as well as jewelry. A 十円玉 JŪ-YEN-DAMA is a 10-yen coin. A 目玉 MEDAMA is an eye-ball, and 目玉燒 MEDAMAYAKI means fried eye-ball-style, which is what you tell the waitress when you want your eggs fried sunny-side up. Sometimes the word egg,TAMAGO,is written 玉子, little-jewel, because this is easier to write than 卵, a picture of two sperms ⊖⊖ , the correct character for egg. 玉 is also used in the name of Japan's oldest and best known domestic wine 赤玉 , AKADAMA, Red-Ball Wine.

The character for jewel 玉 , which is itself formed from the symbol of a king holding the national treasure, encircled by a boundary ▢ is the character for a **country** or a **nation.** The completed character is 国 , pronounced KUNI by itself and KOKU in compounds. An 王国 ŌKOKU is a kingdom and a 国王 KOKUŌ is a king. A 共和国 KYŌWA-KOKU, Joint-Peace-Country, is a Republic.A 外国 GAIKOKU is a foreign land, and a 外国人 GAI-KOKUJIN is a foreigner,an abbreviated form of which is 外人 GAIJIN. KOKU is sometimes used as a suffix in the same way as is the -land in England. 米国 BEIKOKU, Rice-Country, is the Japanese word for America, and 米国人 BEIKOKUJIN the word for an American. The Chinese call America 美国 Beautiful-Country. They call themselves 中国 CHŪGOKU, the Middle Kingdom. The Japanese also call China 中国 CHUGOKU, but they call the section of Japan around Hiroshima 中国 CHŪGOKU also, so some confusion usually results unless the context makes it clear.

A jewel 玉 kept in a treasure house 入 means **treasure.** This character is written 宝 and pronounced TAKARA by itself and HŌ in compounds. A 国宝 KOKUHŌ is a national treasure. 宝石 HŌSEKI, treasure-stones, are jewels. This word is synonymous with, but more eloquent than, 玉 TAMA. Another of the Japanese movie chains is called the 東宝 TŌHŌ, Eastern-Treasure.

The character for king, comprising heaven, earth, man, and ruler 王, with a roof over it 个 means **all, everything, the whole**. It is written 全 and pronounced ZEN. It is used in the names of many organizations to signify the meaning **nation-wide** or **all-**, as in All-Japan Volley-ball Team, All-Japan Coalminers Union, All-Japan National Airways. It is not the ZEN in Zen Buddhism, however.

全日本 ZENNIHON All-Japan.

全米 ZENBEI All-American.

全国 ZENKOKU all-country.This means national,or all-over-the-country.

全体 ZENTAI all-body. This means the whole, entirely.

All buildings under construction have written large upon their walls the sign 安全第一 ANZEN DAIICHI, all-tranquil number-one, which translates as "Safety First."

An ear 耳 next to the mouth 口 of the king 王 is the character for **holy** or **saintly** . The character is written 聖 and pronounced SEI. This is used only in reference to things holy. SEI-Peter is St. Peter, and SEI-Paul is St. Paul. A 聖人 SEIJIN is a Saint, and the 聖書 SEISHO, holy-book, is the Bible.

A character which resembles king 王 and also born 生 is the character for **lord** and **master** . The character for **lord** and **master** , however, is formed from a picture of an altar flame burned in reverence to a god 坴 , and has nothing to do with the origins of the other two. Squared off to final form, **lord** and **master** is written 主 . It is pronounced SHU. One of its most common applications is 主人 SHU-JIN, lord-man, which means master. This is what the Japanese women call their husbands. By extension this character also means **main** or **principal** or **most important.** 主力 SHURYOKU is main force.

Pouring water 氵 on the altar flame 注 forms the character for **pour** . It means **to pour** in general, but has the added meaning of "pour your attention on" or **to concentrate on.** This is pronounced CHŪ. 注意 CHŪI, concentrate-your-mind-on, means pay attention, danger, beware, be careful. This word appears at almost every railroad-crossing, at many intersections, on trucks carrying delicate cargo, and at other danger points. The character 危 , meaning danger, implies that a dangerous situation exists: 注意 implies that if you relax your guard you may be in trouble.

The Chinese knew that a man is master of his

dwelling so they combined man 人 with master 主 to form the character for **dwell** or **live** 住. This is pronounced SUMU by itself and JŪ in compounds. Your 住所 JŪSHO, dwell-place, is your address. The name of one of Japan's largest financial empires is 住友 SUMITOMO, Living-Friend.

To leave your horse 馬 at a dwelling 住 means **to stop or stay somewhere.** When these characters are put together, the man 亻 in dwelling 住 is dropped, and the final form of the character becomes 駐. This is pronounced CHU. To 駐車 CHŪ-SHA, stop-car, is to park your car. A 駐車場 CHŪSHAJŌ is a parking-lot.

The next few characters were taken from pictures of various types of buildings.

In very ancient times, when even a two-storied palace was regarded as high, a picture of a two-storied palace was used to write the character for **high.** This character was first written 髙 and finally 高. It is pronounced TAKAI by itself and KŌ in compounds. This character means high, in any aspect—price, position, or quality. It is also often used in proper names. Some examples are:

高島屋 TAKASHIMAYA High-Island-Shop. A well-known department store on the Ginza.

高松 TAKAMATSU High-Pine. A city on Shikoku which has a famous castle.

高知 KOCHI Lofty-Wisdom. A Prefecture on Shikoku.

A one-story palace 合 was just a **palace**. It was initially written 合 , and later, in its final form, 宮. It is pronounced MIYA by itself and GU in compounds. It means, in addition to **palace,** a **shrine**, mainly for the Shinto religion. A 宮 MIYA, or more usually an O-MIYA, using the honorific O, is a **shrine.** 宮 MIYA is also used in proper names. When the royal family uses it in their name, as they do more often than not, it means **palace-person,** or prince or princess of the royal blood. SUGANOMIYA is Princess Suga, HIRONOMIYA is Prince Hiro. When commoners use MIYA in their names, it means **shrine.** Some examples are:

宮本 MIYAMOTO Shrine-Origin

宮川 MIYAKAWA Shrine-River

宮下 MIYASHITA Below-the-Shrine

It is also used in place names:

大宮 ŌMIYA　　Big-Shrine. A section of Tokyo.

二宮 NINOMIYA　Second-Shrine. A town on the Tokaido.

A house 冂 with the pictograph for enter 入 inside it forms the character for **entered, inside, within** 内 It is pronounced UCHI by itself and NAI in compounds. This character means **inside** in reference to either time or space, and is the equivalent to the English words **within, during, among, between, while.** It is also used in proper names.

内海 NAIKAI　inside-sea. This means Inland Sea. The Seto Inland Sea, or SETO NAIKAI, lies between the islands of Kyushu, Honshu, and Shikoku.

国内 KOKUNAI　inside-the-country. This means domestic. The 日本国内 NIHON KOKU-

NAI Airways is the Japan Domestic Airways.

The character for **same** is a house ☐ with everyone inside speaking with one — mouth ☐ . The final form is 同 , pronounced ONAJI by itself and DŌ in compounds. 共 同 KYŌDŌ, together-same, is the name of Japan's largest news service.

The character for **eat** is formed from a picture of a roof ∧ under which some rice ☐ is being cooked over a fire 火 .These three pictographs were put together first like this 食 , then the shape of fire was changed slightly 火 so that the rice and fire pictographs could be written together with a minimum of pen strokes 良 . The final character is written 食 pronounced TABERU by itself and SHOKU in compounds. When it is pronounced TABERU it is a verb, and in this case always means **to eat.** When used in compounds and pronounced SHOKU it usually means **to eat,** but it can sometimes mean **food** or **meal.** The 夕 食 YŪSHOKU is the evening meal, and 食 品 SHOKUHIN, food-goods, seen on signs at almost all food-store counters, means food.
食 器 SHOKKI   eating-plates.   Cutlery or

tableware.

食人 SHOKUJIN eat-people. This is cannibalism.

The character for **drink** is the character for eat 食 with the addition of a man 人 with his mouth wide open 欠 . The man and mouth are put together like this 欠 . When 食 is used as a building-block it changes shape slightly to 飠 . The final character is 飲 . This is pronounced NOMU by itself, and IN in compounds. Potable-water fountains will usually have the sign 飲水 NOMIMIZU, drinking-water, displayed on them. Bars and coffee shops usually have signs or menus advertising 飲物 NOMIMONO, drinking-things, meaning **beverages.**

This man with his mouth wide open calling out 欠 placed beside the character for two 二 means **next.** This character is written 次, and pronounced TSUGI by itself and JI in compounds. The meaning of this character is extended also to "next in line" or "next in rank." A 次長 JICHŌ, next-chief, is a vice-chief. 次回 JIKAI, next-around, means next time. 次回 is written below some movie ads and posters, meaning "playing next."

A man puffed up with contentment and a full stomach, sleeping siesta-style 𠂉 under a roof 𠆢 signified to the Chinese a **bureaucrat** or **government employee.** They wrote the character first as 宦 and finally 官. This is pronounced KAN. A 長官 CHŌKAN, chief-bureaucrat, is the chief bureaucrat in any government organization. The 次官 JIKAN, next-bureaucrat is the vice-chief bureaucrat. 官 is generally used as a suffix in the title of any government official who has status.

By combining the radicals for bureaucrat 官 and eat 食 the Chinese formed the character for **public building.** In ancient times this character designated buildings used by government officials in their off-duty hours—their official residences, their villas, their commissaries. Now it refers to any public building: art galleries, museums, movie theaters, gymnasiums, meeting halls, libraries. A 別館 BETSUKAN, separate-building, usually abbreviated BEKKAN means annex, while the 本館 HONKAN, main building, is the main building, and the 新館 SHINKAN is the new building. The new wing of the Imperial Hotel is called the SHINKAN. A 会館 KAIKAN, the KAI for which is introduced in the next

paragraph, is a meeting-hall or public hall. It is sometimes translated "building." The well-known 東京
会館 TŌKYŌ KAIKAN, housing several restau-
rants, auditoriums, and several floors of offices, is called in English either **Tokyo Hall** or **Tokyo Building.**

The KAI in KAIKAN, meeting-hall, means **meet.**
The Chinese pictured **meet** as two 二 noses 厶
under one roof 人 . They wrote the final character
会 . This is pronounced AU when used by itself
and KAI in compounds. A 会 KAI is a **meeting** ; AU
means **to meet.**

As we saw above, a 会館 KAIKAN is a Hall or
Building. Some other applications of 会 are:

会場 KAIJŌ meet-place. This is a place
where meetings take place, a
meeting area. It can be indoors
or outdoors. Political meetings, hot-rod meets, dances,
any event where many people
gather together will have the
sign 会場 KAIJŌ posted
at the entrance. There will
usually be, of course, a few
other characters preceding 会

139

場 to tell what kind of meeting is taking place.

会食 KAISHOKU　meet-eat. This is a banquet or a dinner party.

会長 KAICHŌ　meeting-chief. This is the top man in any meeting. Ordinary members of the KAI are called 会員 KAIIN, meeting-members. Many of the bars in downtown Tokyo operate under a 会員 KAIIN system, allowing only 会員 to patronize them.

会話 KAIWA　meet-speak. This means conversation.

協会 KYOKAI　cooperation-association. This is a Society or an Association, The 日米協会, NICHI-BEI KYŌKAI is the Japan-America Society.

A sacrificial altar with the sacrifice atop it 示 was first written 示 and finally 示. The Chinese combined this with the character for earth 土, to form the character 社 meaning, **place where people meet to undertake a social project.** This is pronounced SHA. At first it referred only to a temple, which was the only social project the ancients had, but now it refers to business firms as well. When used in a religious context, 社 means about the same as 宮 MIYA. Both are Shinto Shrines.

会社 KAISHA association-undertaking. This is a business firm or company.

社員 SHAIN undertaking-member. This is a company employee. The white-collar employees of Japanese companies generally give their occupation as 社員

社会 SHAKAI social-association. These are the same two characters which form 会社 KAISHA except reversed. 社会 SHAKAI means society in the sense the sociologists use it— the Great Society; make your way in society; high society

The Japanese word for Corporation is very often abbreviated K.K. when the corporation's name is written in English. K.K. is the abbreviation of 株式会社 KABUSHIKI KAISHA, stock-style association-undertaking. 株 KABU, **stock,** is the only one of these characters we have not already discussed. The origin of 株 is difficult to relate to the modern meaning. It is included here only because you will have an opportunity to see it hundreds of times each day. 株式会社 KABUSHIKI KAISHA will be stamped or printed on almost every product made in Japan. A candy bar, a can of beans, a pocketbook, a pump, a radio will have on it the name of the manufacturer plus 株式会社

The original meaning of 株 KABU, and a meaning which it still retains, is **tree-stump.** If you are walking through the woods and tire a little, you can say "Let's sit down for a while on that KABU." The character for KABU, **stump** or **stock,** is formed from a tree 木 placed beside another tree 木 elaborated into a different form 朱. The reason for the elaboration is too involved to bother with, having to do with a tree in ancient China called the "Red-heart Tree," but you should be able to learn it quickly through constant daily exposure. 株 KABU is now used mainly in relation to corporations and corporate business. A 株主 KABUNUSHI, stock-master, is a stockholder. A 株 KABU is a share of stock.

Another character prominent in the Japanese business world is the one for **business.** The Chinese selected a picture of a merchant opening a box to display his wares 商 to mean **business.** This character was first written 商 then 商 and finally 商 It is pronounced SHŌ. A walk on any busy street will turn up this character many many times. 商店 SHOTEN, business-shop, meaning a mercantile house or a kind of general store, is used frequently in the names of the smaller shops selling miscellaneous goods. A 商店街 SHŌTENGAI, business-shop-street, is a shopping area. Very often merchants get together and put up decorated 商店街 signs at the entrances to their area to publicize their shops. A 商社 SHŌSHA, business-company, is a trading firm, generally for foreign trade, but some local traders also use this in their company name. A trader or a merchant is a 商人 SHŌNIN, and the goods he handles are 商品 SHOHIN.

The character for **God** is composed of the sacrificial altar 示 and a picture of the sun, 日 , where it seems the first deities always resided, with the deity line emanating from the center 申. The completed character is written 神. This is pronounced KAMI by itself and SHIN or JIN in compounds. When 神 is used in reference to a particular God, it is pronounced KAMI, usually followed by the honorific title SAMA, the polite form of Mister. A 神社 JINJA, god-shrine, is a Shinto shrine. A 神宮 JINGŪ is also a shinto shrine, but usually refers to very important shrines, and is often translated as Great or Grand Shrine. The ISE JINGU is the Great Shrine of Ise; the MEIJI JINGU is the Meiji Shrine, named in commemoration of the Emperor Meiji.

The sacrificial altar generally refers to religion, but occasionally it means the sacrificial table itself. An example of this is in the character meaning **prohibited** This character was devised at the time when it was prohibited to enter the king's forest. It is formed from two trees 林 , signifying forest, with a sacrificial altar at its entrance 禁. This inferred that if you entered the forest you would end up on the sacrificial altar. The character is pronounced KIN. 禁止

KINSHI, prohibit-stop, is a popular idiomatic phrase meaning prohibited. Either 禁 KIN or 禁止 KINSHI appears on signs which say No Smoking, No Parking, Please Keep Out, or simply Forbidden. Some of the signs you will frequently see are:

駐車禁止 CHŪSHA KINSHI — Stop-Car Prohibit-Stop. This means No Parking.

立入禁止 TACHIIRI KINSHI — Stand-Enter Prohibit-Stop. This means Entry Prohibited, Keep Out.

禁煙 KIN-EN — Prohibited-Smoking. No Smoking.

右折禁止 USETSU KINSHI — Right-turn-Prohibited. No Right Turn.

The first festivals in China had to do with sacrificial altars. This led the Chinese to construct the character for festival from the sacrificial altar 示 above which a hand 又 holds the sacrificial meat 月. The character was first written 祭, and finally 祭. This is pronounced MATSURI. The verb form of this word, MATSURU, means to **deify** or **make a god out of,** and this may be the way their gods came to be.

A picture of a Chinese drum and cymbal set 🥁, played at all the festivals, became the character for **music** or **pleasure.** This instrument was first drawn 🥁 then finally 楽. When it is used to mean **music,** it is pronounced GAKU. When it is used in the sense of **pleasure,** it is pronounced TANOSHII or RA-KU. Some examples are:

楽 器 GAKKI music-utensil. This is a musical instrument. It should be pronounced GAKUKI, but it is abbreviated to GAKKI to make it easier to say.

音 楽 ONGAKU sound-music. This means music.

楽 is sometimes used in proper names: 有 楽 町 YŪRAKUCHŌ, Have-Pleasure-Town, is the name of the downtown district adjoining the Ginza.

Adding plants 艹 to pleasure 楽 gives the meaning pleasure-plants, **medicine.** The final character is put together like this 薬, and pronounced KUSURI. A 薬 屋 KUSURIYA, medicine-tradesman's, is a drug store. 薬 品 YAKUHIN, medicine-goods, are medical products.

To 祭 MATSURI the Chinese prefixed a picture of a terraced mountainside 畠, written first 𝄐 then 𝄐 and finally 阝, indicating the border of the territory in which their festivals were held, to form the character for **boundary** or **border** 際. This is pronounced SAI. 国 際 KOKUSAI, country-boundary, means international.

The pictograph for terraced mountainside 阝 is another one which cannot be used as a character by itself, but must be combined with other pictographs to form a character. It brings to the character the meaning of terraced mountainside, or a series of levels. An example of this is the character that means the **floors of a building, rank,** or **grade.** The Chinese formed this character from 阝 plus the character for **all** or **everybody.** The character for **everybody** is composed of two seated men 比比, representing "this man" and "that man", and a nose 自, representing "me". **Everybody** is written 皆 and pronounced MINA or MINNA. The character for **rank,** or **grade,** or **floor of a building** is written 階 and pronounced KAI. The elevator girls will call out the floors like this:

一 階 IKKAI First floor. This should be pronounced ICHI-KAI, but it is always shortened to IKKAI.

二 階 NIKAI Second floor

三 階 SANGAI Third floor

The next few characters are related to the weather. The Chinese pictured **rain** as raindrops falling from a cloud. They wrote it first, then and finally. It is pronounced AME.

An **umbrella** was first drawn, and then some people were added to complete the picture. The final character looks like this. It is pronounced KASA, and means **umbrella**.

The falling rain combined with a picture of a broom means **snow**. The broom was abbreviated first then. The final form of this character is, although it is now sometimes written. In either form it is pronounced YUKI.

A streak of lightning amidst the falling rain formed the character for **lightning**. The Chinese first drew the lightning streak like this, then

卫 and finally 电 . The completed character is 電 , pronounced DEN. For the first few thousand years after the Chinese invented this character it meant **lightning**. Then it was discovered that lightning held electricity. Since the Chinese and the Japanese at the time had no word for electricity, they selected 電 DEN to fill this need. 電 now means either **lightning** or **electricity.**

As various electric machines and products were invented, new compounds were needed to name these things. The Chinese and Japanese, in most cases, just added 電 DEN to other appropriate descriptive characters and coined new words:

電 車 DENSHA electric-car. This is a streetcar or trolley.

電 線 DENSEN electric-line. This is an electric wire.

電 力 DENRYOKU electric-power. The 東京電力株式会社 TŌKYŌ DENRYOKU KABUSHIKI KAISHA is the Tokyo Electric Power Company.

電 話 DENWA electric-speaking. This is a telephone.

The Chinese pictured vapor as a few ephemeral lines 〰. They later drew them 气 and finally 气. This is the vapor pictograph, to which the Chinese added other pictographs to show what kind of vapor was implied. Adding the character for rice 米, which gave the vapor life, formed the new character 氣, meaning **spirit** or **energy**. This is pronounced KI. 電氣 DENKI, lightning-energy, is the formal word for electricity. A 氣体 KITAI, vapor-body, is a gas. In modern times, this character is sometimes shortened to 気.

Vapor 气, with the pictograph for water 氵 forms the character for water-vapor, **steam**. The completed character is written 汽 and pronounced KI. A 汽車 KISHA steam-car, is a train.

The character for ground 土 with two dots inside to represent the ore 圡 under a mound to show great quantity △ means **metal**. It was written first 金 and then in final form 金. This character was also extended to mean the primary metal, **gold**, and further, to mean **money.** It is pronounced KIN or KANE. 金曜日 KINYŌBI, metal-day, is Friday. A 金魚 KINGYO is a gold-fish. A 金庫 KINKO, money-storehouse, is a safe.

The character for eye 目 combined with the character for compare 比 forms the character for comparing-eyes, staring eyeball-to-eyeball, meaning **to be equal.** This character was first written 昆 then 昆 and finally, for ease in writing, it was abbreviated to 艮 . Then. combining the character **to be equal** with the character for **gold**, the character for **silver** 銀 was formed. This is pronounced GIN. A 銀行 GINKŌ, silver- go, is a bank. The 日本銀行 NIHON GINKŌ is the Bank of Japan. 東京銀行新宿支店 TŌKYŌ GINKŌ SHINJUKU-SHITEN is the Shinjuku Branch of the Bank of Tokyo. 水銀 SUIGIN liquid-silver, is mercury.

The character for **seat** the Chinese formed from a picture of two people 人人 seated on the ground 土 under a shed 广 . The final character was put together like this 座 . It is pronounced ZA. This character is also extended to mean a **place where people gather.** In this sense it is used in the names of many theaters. The 有楽座 YŪRAKUZA is the Yuraku Theater. A 名画座 MEIGAZA, masterpiece-theater, is an Art Theater. The KABUKIZA of course is the Kabuki Theater. The 銀 座 GINZA, silver-seat, is Tokyo's fabulous Ginza.

In recent times, particularly after the second world war, simplified forms of a few of the characters have been developed. Some of these new forms are officially recognized by the Japanese Government while others are simply popular forms of printing. Both the original and the simplified forms are in current use, even though the Government is trying to limit use to the simplified forms for the ones they have approved. There should be no difficulty in recognizing the simplified form since the simplifications have usually been limited to minor changes, as for example replacing a series of dots with one straight line or representing everything inside a frame by an x.

The simplified forms of the characters presented in READ JAPANESE TODAY are:

	original character	simplified form
mother	母	毋
every	每	毎
sea	海	海
poison	毒	毒

	original character	simplified form
ward	區	区
struggle	爭	争
learning	學	学
hurry	急	急
sell	賣	売
burn	燒	焼
bad	惡	悪
undertaking	社	社
god	神	神
spirit	氣	気

There are two sets of kana, each set containing 46 letters. One set is called Hiragana and the other is called Katakana, and each set contains identical sounds to the other. As a general practice, the Hiragana are used to form the grammatical endings and the Katakana are used to write in Japanese the foreign words the Japanese have borrowed.

Each kana is a syllable rather than a letter, and most kana are combinations of one consonant and one vowel. These syllables are formed basically by adding each of the vowels A, I, U, E and O to each of the consonants K, S, T, N, H, M, Y, R and W. The A, I, U, E and O sounds themselves and the N sound complete each set of kana.

The exceptions to this pattern are first that the syllable SI is replaced by SHI, the syllable TI replaced by CHI, and the syllable TU replaced by TSU (the sounds SI, TI and TU do not exist in Japanese), and second that the syllables YI, YE, WI, WU and WE are no longer used.

This is the Hiragana Chart:

COLUMN / LINE	A	I	U	E	O
SINGLE VOWEL	あ A	い I	う U	え E	お O
K	か KA	き KI	く KU	け KE	こ KO
S	さ SA	し SHI	す SU	せ SE	そ SO
T	た TA	ち CHI	つ TSU	て TE	と TO
N	な NA	に NI	ぬ NU	ね NE	の NO
H	は HA	ひ HI	ふ HU	へ HE	ほ HO
M	ま MA	み MI	む MU	め ME	も MO
Y	や YA		ゆ YU		よ YO
R	ら RA	り RI	る RU	れ RE	ろ RO
W	わ WA		ん N		を O

This is the Katakana Chart:

COLUMN / LINE	A	I	U	E	O
SINGLE VOWEL	ア A	イ I	ウ U	エ E	オ O
K	カ KA	キ KI	ク KU	ケ KE	コ KO
S	サ SA	シ SHI	ス SU	セ SE	ソ SO
T	タ TA	チ CHI	ツ TSU	テ TE	ト TO
N	ナ NA	ニ NI	ヌ NU	ネ NE	ノ NO
H	ハ HA	ヒ HI	フ HU	ヘ HE	ホ HO
M	マ MA	ミ MI	ム MU	メ ME	モ MO
Y	ヤ YA		ユ YU		ヨ YO
R	ラ RA	リ RI	ル RU	レ RE	ロ RO
W	ワ WA		ン N		ヲ O

In addition to the sounds which appear in the preceding charts, other sounds are formed in one of two ways: by combining two or more kana to form one syllable, or by adding either two small lines (called nigori) or a small circle (called maru) to certain of the kana to change their pronunciation slightly.

Examples of the first method are the adding of any of the single vowels to a kana to form the long vowels, or the adding of the Y-line syllables, や, ゆ, or よ, to the I column syllables to form syllables of the pattern KYA, KYU, or KYO. The syllable TŌ is written と う, and the syllable KYŌ is written き ょ う.

An example of the second method is the forming of the syllables begining with the consonants G, Z, D, B and P. Adding nigori to the K-line か き く け こ forms the G-line:

が	ぎ	ぐ	げ	ご
GA	GI	GU	GE	GO

Adding nigori to the S-line forms the Z-line:

ざ	じ	ず	ぜ	ぞ
ZA	JI	ZU	ZE	ZO